WELLS CATHEDRAL

WELLS CATHEDRAL

BY

R. D. REID

PUBLISHED BY THE
FRIENDS OF WELLS CATHEDRAL

FIRST PUBLISHED 1963

REVISED 1973

© *R. D. Reid 1973*

PRINTED IN GREAT BRITAIN
in 10 point Baskerville type
BY THE FAITH PRESS LTD.
LEIGHTON BUZZARD LU7 7NQ
ISBN 0 902321 11 0

CONTENTS

INTRODUCTION

IN the early years of this century an excellent guide book existed for the benefit of visitors and indeed of scholars interested in Wells Cathedral. This was Dr Percy Dearmer's volume in *Bell's Cathedral Series,* which, under a modest format, provided much reliable and readable information. The value of this book was further enhanced by revision, in 1921, under the supervision of Dean Armitage Robinson, who added some sections. It has long been out of print. Since 1946, the 'Friends of Wells Cathedral' have published a series of valuable monographs on such subjects as the 'Statuary of the West Front,' the 'Organs' and the 'Glass.' The latter, in particular, contains a summary of the meticulous examination made by Dean Woodforde. At the same time the need has long been felt for a comprehensive guide which would, as it were, tie together this somewhat haphazard information; and perhaps fill in some gaps. My thanks are due, firstly, to Dean Woodforde who kindly read the manuscript for me. Indeed it was written at his instigation, and to that extent he is to blame for it, although not for its errors or opinions. The chief labour of help and criticism, however, has fallen upon the capable shoulders of the Chancellor of the Cathedral, Dr D. S. Bailey and upon those of Mr K. C. A. Wills, Secretary of the 'Friends of the Cathedral,' who, by their detailed criticism have saved me from many errors and omissions and to whom I am deeply grateful. The Master Mason, Mr W. A. Wheeler, has been ready to answer a multitude of questions, and the Verger's staff under Mr Rice has always tolerated and indeed encouraged my penetration into the remote corners of the great building. A review of sources of information has been given in Note 1, p. 130.

Revision of 1973
For this I am much indebted to Mr L. S. Colchester for information and help, and again to the Reverend K. C. A. Wills for his careful scrutiny of the text.

Wells.   R. D. REID

CHAPTER I

THE EARLY CHURCHES AT WELLS

THE history of Wells is the history of its church. There are no signs of occupation before the eighth century by natives, or by Roman or other invaders. This is perhaps surprising when we remember the early story of the Mendip Hills, the cave dwellers of Wookey Hole, and the lake villagers of the moors. Wells, it seems, was a blind spot in a busy neighbourhood and this can probably be explained by the fact that there were no obvious means of defence. But as soon as life became more settled, it must have appeared a desirable site, well above the floor level of the moors, below the wilderness of the Mendip Forest and with, as its name implies, an abundance of water.

It is supposed that a church, probably collegiate, was established by King Ina of the West Saxons about A.D. 700[1]. Another reason for the choice of the site was the fact that it was, unlike Bath, more or less in the centre of the county.[2] We know too that the King was often hunting at Cheddar and was concerned with the enlargement of the church at Glastonbury. He must frequently have passed this way.

The history of the first church, until the certain establishment of the bishopric in 909, remains obscure. The unreliable nature of early accounts is shown by the fact that they mostly postulate a bishopric of Somerset at Congresbury from about A.D. 170 until it was removed by a Bishop Daniel to Wells about 700. There can be little truth in this story, although the existence of a bishopric of Somerset at Wells from 700 to 909 is indicated in the alleged charter granted to Glastonbury by King Ina in 725 and quoted by William of Malmesbury : *Hoc etiam provideat idem Episcopus ut singulis annis cum clericis suis qui Fontanetum sunt.*[3] However, William of Malmesbury's writings on the early history of Glastonbury are very suspect, and this reference does not say that the bishop actually lived at Wells. On the other hand there seems to be no particular reason why such a reference should have been invented, as there was for the publication of legends concerning Glastonbury itself. William was living with kind hosts in the abbey at Glastonbury when he wrote in 1125, and may have felt some obligation to enhance the reputation of the house, and so encourage pilgrims.

A considerable variety of early names for Wells are found. We see Fontanetum above, and in addition to the obvious Welve and Wielia, Godwin[4] gives Fonticuli: *Villa a copia fonticulum sic dicta.* Tidington is given in a charter of Edward the Confessor.[5] Then we find Cideston in *Historiola*,[1] probably the same as Tydeston of *Historia Minor*.[1] Camden has Theodorodunum. It is not impossible that Tydeston was the name of an earlier hill settlement to the south-east of Wells. Dean Robinson[6] quotes the use of the word Tidesput as an eastern boundary in a town charter of 1200, and 'Tithesput furlang' as being on the east of the bishop's garden in 1245. The same name was used of a close in the manor of Wells in 1539. The field adjoining the bishop's garden on the east is now called Torfurlong. On its south is Tor Hill and King's Castle, the nearest point to Wells with a prehistoric settlement.

THE SAXON BISHOPRIC OF SOMERSET

When we come to the year 909, speculation may justifiably cease, as the foundation of the bishopric about that time has never been questioned. The evidence was fully examined by Dean Robinson[7] who concludes that the only fact in doubt is the date, which may possibly be 910. Ten years after the death of King Alfred, Plegmund, the Archbishop of Canterbury, with the help of King Edward the Elder rearranged the Wessex dioceses. He divided Winchester, setting up another bishopric at Ramsbury. Sherborne, which had also come out of Winchester in 705, was divided into three by the creation of the Somerset diocese at Wells, and another for Devon at Crediton.[8] The first Bishop of Wells was Athelm, who was educated at Glastonbury. His brother, Heorstan, father of St Dunstan was known to have an estate near that place. It is likely that they were all relatives of the king. We know little of the work of Athelm at Wells, but he was an able man, and was translated to Canterbury on the death of the aged Plegmund in 923. It fell to him the very next year to crown the new king, Athelstan, and incidentally to introduce his nephew Dunstan, aged 14, to the court. He only survived at Canterbury for another year when his successor at Wells, Wulfhelm, was also translated to the metropolitan see. It is said that Wulfhelm undertook the dangerous journey to Rome in 927 to receive the pallium in person. On his return he consecrated a successor, Ælfeah, to Wells. Wulfhelm died at Canterbury in 942. Thus the first two bishops of Wells were buried in the Saxon cathedral there, and it is thought that they rest near the altar of St Martin in the later cathedral. Ælfeah died in 938, and was probably buried at Wells, but we have no record of his tomb. There succeeded a second Wulfhelm, 938–55. Of Brihthelm who came to Wells in 956, there is a story that he went to Canterbury to be enthroned as Archbishop when the king died; and Dunstan was chosen by the new King Edgar in his place. He is the first certainly to be buried at Wells. Florence of Worcester says: *Sumertunensi episcopus Brihthelmus obiit et in Wyllum humatus est*.[9] This was in 973. The importance of Wells at this time is shown by the fact that the first five bishops were so closely connected with the king and the primatial see of Canterbury.

Cyneward became bishop of Wells in 974 to die a year later, ten days before King Edgar, with whose name he is linked in the Anglo-Saxon Chronicle. The next bishop was an Abbot of Glastonbury, one Sigar. He ruled at Wells for twenty-two years, and by many authorities was thought to have been the first bishop.

Sigar's is the earliest episcopal tomb in the cathedral, being the first going eastward along the north choir aisle. The effigies over the tombs of the Saxon bishops now in the choir aisles were made by Bishop Jocelin after he had brought back the episcopal seat from Bath in 1206.[10]

He collected the bones and placed them in wooden boxes, not apparently too carefully, as one box now contains nearly two skeletons. He also had their names beautifully cast in lead plates and placed in the boxes. Thus, under the tomb of Sigar there is a box of bones and a plate: *Sigarus Epc Wellensis*. The seven existing Saxon tombs form a uniform series, and it is evident that they were constructed, and the bones boxed and labelled, before Jocelin himself was buried amongst them in 1242. Thus they form a record of his spiritual ancestors in the ancient see of his birthplace, to which he restored the dignity filched from it by Bath.

These Saxon tombs have been described in very great detail by Dr Fryer.[11] Recent generations treated them very badly so that they got completely muddled, and two effigies were at one time in the undercroft. Dean Robinson, † 1933, with great care, and after a full review of the evidence, restored them to their original positions. He provided the present bases to hold the bones and tablets. The first five tombs as now identified unfortunately do not correspond with documentary lists, and we can only conclude that Jocelin's information was faulty. He very likely relied on oral traditions as to the identity of the remains he found and then so carefully boxed and labelled. He either thought that Sigar was the first bishop, or could find no remains for earlier ones and so did not provide monuments. Sigar's tomb, and that of Bishop Eilwinus are clearly defined. There is a tomb with a lost label, making three. The remaining two of this series are marked from their tablets as Burwoldus and Levericus. A portion of a stone inscription to 'Burwoldus' was also found and is incorporated with the existing inscription. We can only speculate as to the identity of these two bishops, as their names do not appear in any of the accepted lists. All the figures are under canopies and are vested in Mitre with Staff (no Sudery), Chasuble, Dalmatic (no Tunicle), Alb, Maniple and Amice. They are attributed to the early part of the thirteenth century. The effigy of Bishop Sigar has a peculiar ornamentation to the top of the chasuble and Dr Fryer considers that this is meant to represent a separate circlet and is in fact an example of the *super humerale episcoporum* which may have been derived from the morse or ephod worn by the High Priest in the Jewish Temple.

Dean Robinson has pointed out that Brihtwig was the last of a series of scholar bishops, usually promoted abbots. There follows a long list of appointments at Wells, as elsewhere, from amongst court chaplains and other clergy personally known to the king. Wells, however, was fortunate, as the next two bishops under the Saxon regime each ruled for long periods, Dudoc from 1033 to 1060, and Giso from 1060 to 1088. The former was an Old Saxon from Saxony, obviously an able administrator, obtaining for the church the estates of Congresbury and Banwell. Giso was a native of Lorraine, and, not being of Saxon birth, he remained undisturbed at the Conquest, thus bringing a measure of security to the see in a troublous period. He drew the canons together into a community, and built accommodation for them, maybe on the site of the present palace or just north of it.

The tombs of these two 'last of the Saxons' are different from the five already described. It is generally accepted that they were made sometime, perhaps twenty years, after the others. There are no canopies and the figures are more lifelike and give less of an impression that they were cut out of a flat block of stone. Leaf foliage adorns the slabs and the heads rest on pillows. There is a remarkable difference in the mitres which, unlike the others, are of the true Saxon type, so low in fact that writers as late as Britton, 1829, mistook them for priests' caps. The infulae are plain and not fringed. It is known that these two bishops were buried on either side of the High Altar in the Saxon cathedral in places of honour, Dudoc on the south and Giso on the north, and the suggestion is that Jocelin found their tombs in place in the new cathedral. He did not at first make new ones for them as he did for their predecessors. Then, as time went on and they appeared shabby he completed the series. Maybe, although this seems unlikely, there were older effigies, with the low type of mitre, which he copied. Perhaps his knowledge of ecclesiology improved.

It should be noted that the High Altar in Jocelin's time was in line with the present throne, and that the tombs were later moved eastwards to their present positions. Another sign of fourteenth century change is that the leaden plate of the doubtful Bishop Levericus was made new at that time, and this may have caused confusion. Dean Robinson suggests that the other 'intruding' bishop, Burwold, was confused with Brihtwold, Bishop of Wilts, or Burhwold, Bishop of Cornwall.

These bishops may have been commemorated in the martyrology used at Wells, and so only the day of their death and not the year would be known when Jocelin made his investigations.

NORMAN BISHOPS OF BATH

As was to be expected, the next appointment after Giso was of a thoroughgoing Norman, John de Villula, a native of Tours and a physician. The interesting suggestion has been made that he was practising at Bath. It was a sad day however for Wells. Bishop John was not content with transferring the see to Bath, but he destroyed the buildings erected for the canons at Wells by Giso. He built a country house for himself on the site, and the clergy were once more compelled to live *cum populo communiter*.

Having obtained a grant of the town of Bath from the king, he set up there the system of a cathedral priory. The bishop lived in the monastic community as abbot, but the monk elected to the second place as prior had more extensive powers than in other houses, and is always shown vested as an abbot with staff and mitre. When a century later the bishops returned to Wells, the house at Bath remained a priory until the reformation. The status of the church at Wells meanwhile becomes very obscure. The canons and other clergy lived under a provost, but we have no certain information that the bishops were enthroned here as well as at Bath, or that the canons had any say in their election. Wells really ceased to be a cathedral church, and so continued under the next Bishop of Bath, Godfrey, 1123–35.

A change however came about with the appointment of Robert, who was a monk of Lewes, although born in Normandy. He must have been a remarkable man. He not only finished the great Norman cathedral at Bath of which evident traces remain, but did much to restore Wells to its former dignity. In particular he granted the charter which virtually set up the body of the Dean and Chapter as we know it to-day, and secured much property to it.

It is remarkable that soon after the bishopric had been removed to Bath, the bishops cast longing eyes at the ancient seat at Wells, and began the work of restoration, which was completed by the 'English' bishop Jocelin, who eventually left Bath. This raises an important and insoluble question. Where did Jocelin find the original tombs which he thus reconstructed, or in other words where was the site of the Saxon Cathedral? There seem to be only two possible answers. It was either here on the spot where the cathedral of *c.* 1180 was subsequently built, or a short distance to the south in the Camery churchyard. The first inference is the most obvious, but no positive evidence remains. Whether excavations will be permitted in the future or whether they would yield any results is problematical. We have then to consider the other alternative. A visitor who goes out into the Camery and turns back to look at the cloister wall will see evident signs of two buildings which have been erected against it, but which are now destroyed. They are of the thirteenth and fifteenth centuries, but, from a consideration of the masonry and form of buttress, the wall itself is thought to be older, i.e. of the twelfth century. Because of the obvious interest of the site, extensive excavations were carried out in the churchyard in 1890. The plan of the perpendicular chantry chapel built by Bishop Stillington was soon revealed and more will be said of this later. Beneath were the remains of an Early English building, but the remarkable fact emerged that this was constructed at an angle of 12° north of east, quite out of line with the later buildings.[12] In other words, while the east wall of the cloister formed a square west end to Stillington's chapel, it must have made an awkward and slanting termination to the earlier building. Now the existence of this earlier chapel is well documented from 1250 onwards as the Chapel of the Blessed Mary, *juxta claustrum*.[13] In spite of its peculiar position, it was the much used Lady Chapel of the cathedral. We will call it in future Lady Chapel I.[14] The inference drawn from the excavations was that this Early English chapel had been erected upon the site of a building much earlier than the cloister wall or indeed of any of the existing buildings. Otherwise it would not be at this awkward angle and in this peculiar place. It seems likely that it was built upon the site of the Saxon Lady Chapel. We have references also to this chapel when it was endowed by Bishop Giso, and restored in 1196.[15] Following this reasoning we would expect the Saxon Cathedral itself to lie west of the chapel at an angle, across the existing fifteenth century cloisters, so that its west end would come close to the Market Place. Unfortunately excavation of this area, although attempted, proved difficult owing to modern graves, and was abandoned. One undoubted Saxon Stone, with interlacing carving, was found in the Camery, and is preserved in the cathedral library. It is very similar to the shaft of the fine cross in West Camel church in the diocese.[16] Later Sir William St John Hope reviewed the evidence, and produced a further argument in favour of this southern site.[17] If the ordnance map of Wells be examined it will be found that all the ancient streets are orientated with this old building. The new cathedral, although more nearly East-West, is quite out of line with the town. Moreover we would expect the High Street to lead directly to the west door of the cathedral. This it would do to the old building, and plainly does not to the present one, which faces a field or cemetery. It seems not unlikely that Bishop Reginald, when he began building in 1180, moved to the north because of trouble with the wells or springs. Even so, there was much disturbance to the foundations of the central tower and to this day there is cause for anxiety at the east end of the cathedral. The city of Wells is unique in that it is built not on the banks of a river but on its source. It is honeycombed with underground channels.[18] The St Andrew's Stream, or the Water of Wells, flowed south-west from the great well and may have determined the peculiar orientation of the Saxon Cathedral and later Lady Chapel standing upon its banks. When we enquire what was done to the Saxon Cathedral, we are frustrated. Typical is the statement of the seventeenth century writer Wharton which says that Bishop Robert *dedicavit ecclesiam Wellensem. Multas ruinas destructionem ejus in pluribus locis comminantes, egregie reparavit.*[19] Godwin is equally contradictory : 'he pulled down a great part of it and repaired it.' Until recently, all writers have taken the testimony of the *Historiola* as final : *Ecclesia Welliae suo consilio fabricata est, et auxilio. Et factum est, cum perfecta*

*esset ecclesia Welliae ab eodem domino Welliae ascitis sibi et
adjunctis grandis et praeclarae memoriae tribus pontificibus.*
There follows a description of the consecration and dedication
of the church in the presence of these three bishops, Hereford,
Worcester, and Salisbury.[20]

It does seem however improbable that Robert should have
been building a great Norman cathedral at Bath, much larger
than the present 'abbey,' and another at Wells. We know that
he must have started almost from scratch at Bath since a
fire destroyed all the work of Bishop John in 1140. The choir
of this great building extended over what is now the Orange
Grove into the river gardens beyond. The Norman bishops of
the see were buried therein, and it is perhaps poetic justice
that their tombs now lie under the streets, whereas those of
their Saxon predecessors at Wells are still carefully tended.
If a Norman cathedral had in fact also been built at Wells
we should expect to find *some* trace of it, whereas not a
single stone remains. Dean Robinson is reported to have seen
one but it cannot now be found.[21] As Dr Bilson has pointed
out, the present cathedral has all the appearances of having
been laid out afresh on a virgin site. The measurements are
perfect, and there are no distortions or attempts to use old
foundations. It is difficult to believe that a Norman cathedral
could have vanished without a trace. Altogether it would
seem that these early writers—and they are demonstrably in
error in other respects—have laid the emphasis on rebuilding,
when it should have been on repairing, the Saxon church.

There was a gap of eight years after Bishop Robert's death
in 1166 before Reginald de Bohun, son of Bishop Jocelin of
Sarum, was enthroned in 1174[22] as Bishop of Bath.

NEW BUILDING AT WELLS

We must next consider the rather vexed question of the
date for the commencement of the present building. No one
would now subscribe to the statement of Collinson [23] that 'the
greater part was built in the year 1239.' The first serious study
of dating was made by Canon Church,[24] and he considered
that building began soon after the arrival of Bishop Reginald
in 1174. This view was more or less accepted until 1929 when

B

Dean Robinson and Dr Bilson examined afresh the evidence of the documents and the building respectively. The former concluded that the date cannot have been later than 1186, and the latter that it was after 1190.[25] Bilson relies considerably upon comparison with Glastonbury, where we have a firm date in that the abbey was entirely destroyed by fire in 1184. Rebuilding began at once with the Lady Chapel at the western end, on the site of the wattle church. The walls of this remain, and Bilson formed the conclusion that they must be older than the choir at Wells. Apart from a general profusion of ornament due to a desire to honour this very holy spot, the Lady Chapel exhibits two notable characteristics: (1) the windows are round headed; (2) there is a copious use of insets of Blue Lias with the Doulting stone. At first sight the round-headed windows indicate a date previous to the lancets at Wells, but further examination shows such elaborate detail that it seems likely that we have a deliberate archaism for this very special building. If construction at Wells really began five years later we would certainly expect to find that the use of insets had been copied. There is no trace of them in the first phase of building here, whereas they were used to excess in later work, following the example of Glastonbury. A date for the first work at Wells would seem to be early in the ninth decade of the twelfth century, and this agrees with the documentary evidence.

CHAPTER II

THE EARLY ENGLISH CHURCH
THIRTEENTH-CENTURY CHOIR AND TRANSEPTS

THE first cruciform church at Wells was clearly laid out as a whole, i.e. a choir of three bays, transepts of the same, and a nave of indeterminate length, soon after 1180 or, if a later date be preferred, 1190. We would expect work to begin with the choir, and there are indications that it did. There is, however, little difference in the work of transepts and choir, except that added dignity is given to the latter by a greater width of each bay. A glance will show that the existing choir was doubled in length in the fourteenth century and that, inside the Early English portion, little of the original work remains visible above the pier arches. The hood moulding of these, together with the heads which probably stopped it, has been sliced off. Also, part of the outline of the old triforium arches, now filled in, may be seen near the crossing. The capitals of the arcade are less deep than those elsewhere in the church and the foliage carving is rather elementary and varies from capital to capital as if some uniform style was being sought. (A portion of the first pier capital facing the north aisle was renewed in the fourteenth century.)

The question arises as to the nature of the Early English east end, which has now vanished. On the outside of these first three bays of the choir the old work goes right up to roof level ending in a plain corbel table typical of the period. Larger fourteenth century clerestory windows have been clumsily inserted beneath the old drip stones. If we look at the *aisle* walls, we notice again the insertion of Decorated windows, although in more seemly fashion, but the old work continues for four, and not three, bays eastward from the crossing. The wall is much thicker than the newer work farther east, and there is a larger buttress at the end of the fourth bay. This means that the aisles were returned round the rectangular east end behind the High Altar. The only church remaining with an Early English east end of this

period intact is to be found at Abbey Dore. This seems to be
a few years later than Wells, and was begun perhaps about
1190. It has a double eastern aisle, one vaulted section forming an ambulatory, the other, farther east, with a row of
five altars. A lean-to roof covers both aisles. There is no
projecting chapel. At Wells the end aisle seems to have been
of the same width as those north and south, but it would
have been wide enough to hold altars and to allow for a
processional path.

We have some evidence of this arrangement from the
vaulting shafts of the older aisles which spring from the
wall bench. The first two on either side have been retained
intact, including their capitals, to hold the later vault. In
the north aisle the third triplet curiously appears in two
vertical parts, including the 'water-holding' base.

There are two shafts in one part to the west, and one in
the other. The whole capital has been renewed. This shows
clearly that a corner existed at this point as if to end the
aisle, and that a respond of two shafts has been expanded
into a triplet. There is the same sort of indication in the
south choir aisle. Here all the shafts and the capital have
been renewed, but the base remains cut in two portions, one
for a corner. The only possible conclusion is that the side
aisles ended at this point in line with the High Altar, and
that one entered the eastern aisle through an arch. There is,
however, a serious objection to this conclusion in that no
sign remains in the aisle walls, of the attachment of such a
transverse wall containing arches. The courses are perfect.

One bay farther east, however, where we know from evidence outside that the main wall did cross over, there is clearly
much disturbance of the courses.

It has been concluded by Willis and Church that this final
wall was broken in the middle behind the High Altar to give
entrance to a large rectangular Lady Chapel (II). A tentative
plan is given by Church. In 1914 Dean Robinson caused
excavations to be made on this site under the existing choir,
but they were inconclusive.[26] It must be emphasized that a
Lady Chapel certainly existed hereabouts in the thirteenth

century, but the altar may have been the centre one of the series in the aisle.[27]

There is no evidence of a large protruding chapel, and the Dore arrangement seems the more likely. At the south end of this east aisle a small window with two-centred arch has been filled in, as may be seen outside and inside the church. This was above the bench and below the main window, but was not in the centre of the bay, being nearer a presumed altar. It looks like an authentic example of a Low Side Window, although one has never before been found in a cathedral. The private chapel of the bishop in the palace at Wells, however, possesses one of much the same date and shape as this. The purpose of these windows is still uncertain, and some fifteen suggestions have been made, of which two seem reasonable and generally acceptable : (a) ventilation, (b) the ringing of a sacring bell to inform people outside of the moment of the Elevation. The latter use would apply more to a parish church, and so both these examples at Wells provide some evidence in favour of alternative (a).

Unless further excavation takes place we shall probably never know the form of the eastern arcade at Wells. It must either have been of three arches like Abbey Dore and the recently discovered east end of Glastonbury or, as Bilson suggested, two arches with a central pier behind the High Altar. Above and below the high vault there was almost certainly a triplet of lancet windows. It would seem likely that the extension choir was completed before the old east wall was removed. A considerable amount of cross-hatched ashlar was then available, and we find this built into the present High Altar screen and the south screen of the choir.

THE TRANSEPTS—OUTSIDE THE CHURCH

Of the transepts, the south appears to be the older, having a rugged Romanesque appearance on the outside, lacking the elaborate arcade of rolled arches we find on the north. This difference may not however be due to age, but to a desire to supply greater ornament to the more public front on the north. Outside, the gable end of the south transept is plain save for a triplet window to the loft. The centre panel of this

is blank. Below are two string courses above the large triple
lancet. This has a plain hood mould continued to meet the
buttresses. Below, again, is a plain arcade of six rolled arches
standing upon a string course. The tops of the centre four
were cut off when the window was lowered in the fifteenth
century. Three separate lancets with sills on a string course
nine feet from the ground completes the main south face.

The corner buttresses are plain massive affairs in three
stages, with octagonal pinnacles and caps. The only ornament
is at the third stage, which has attached shafts with floriated
capitals at the corners. Such shafts are also used on the North
Porch which seems to show that the latter is of early date,
say before 1200.

There are no pinnacles on the corner buttresses to the
aisles, which rise in two stages. At both sides of the transept
the three clerestory lancets have hood moulding, returned
right round the simple clasping type buttresses between them.
These rise in two very shallow stages, the second reaching
the cornice. Only one clerestory buttress is required at each
side and this is connected with its aisle buttress by a flyer
under the steeply pitched lead roof. The slopes between the
stages, however, have been replaced at various times right
round the cathedral, and it is inadvisable to attempt dating
in this way. The lofts of the transept aisles are lit by exceptionally large lancets at their ends. There was a small lean-to
vestry at the south end of the east aisle, no doubt serving
the altars within. Remains of the doorway may be seen
inside, and the roof marks outside. A similar vestry existed
for the north transept, and its door now gives entrance to
the Chapter House stairs.

If we consider the exterior of the north transept we find
it considerably more ornate. The north-eastern buttress is
obscured by the later Chapter House stairs, and that on the
west somewhat modified in appearance in that it provides
a mounting for a clock face. The first two stages of the main
north transept face are plain, like those on the south, except
for string courses. The second stage is also similar, with an
arcade of arches carried right across the face, some cut off
by the later window. The third stage at clerestory level, how-

ever, has an arcade which is absent on the south transept, but here carried along the face, including the buttresses. Each face of the latter has two arches, and the northern is continued in this way for one unit on the wall of the transept itself. Three arches then follow as part of the arcade, but much wider, taking the triplet lancet window. One more blank unit follows until the other buttress is reached, and the arcade continues round it. The two outer windows of the main triplet are at a lower level and the blank spaces thus left under the arcade are filled with circles of foliage carving. The pinnacles on the corner buttresses have an exactly similar, but smaller arcade, three arches to each face; and this is carried across the gable end of the transept in twelve units. Finally there are square faced second stage pinnacles with two arches to each face, and hexagonal caps.

The corner buttresses to the aisles of the north transept are interesting. They go up in one stage from plinth to parapet relieved only by the string course and hood mould of the windows continued round them. So they appear very similar to Norman clasping buttresses. At parapet level there is an octagonal pinnacle, capped, and with the usual arcade of arches. There are no such pinnacles on the south transept.

THE TRANSEPTS—INSIDE THE CHURCH

Inside the transepts we find similar piers to those in the choir, except that they are much closer together, and the resulting arches more acute. The triforium stage consists of pairs of arched openings with mouldings continuous from jamb to arch in outer and inner orders. There is an intermediate order to the arch, making three in all, and this carries a bold chamfer returned as a sill. A plain hood mould is also continued to the base. The absence of any break or capital to the arches is the outstanding feature of the triforium, and indeed of much of Reginald's church. The clerestory stage is very lofty, with blank masonry for nine feet above the passage floor before the window sill is reached. The windows were, of course, plain lancets, tracery being added in the fifteenth century. They have hood mouldings

inside, stopped with labels of simple carving. There are deep
rere arches.

The shafts of the high vault originate in corbels at the base
of the triforium stage, thus dividing this stage into bays. The
effect is quite different from that in the nave, where the
corbels are placed above the continuous run of triforium
arches. This triplet of shafts, of which the centre one is
keeled, continues upwards to a capital with a squared abacus
from which spring the ribs of the vault. The south and north
walls of the transepts contain, of course, no vaulting shafts
and so a continuous run of triforium openings is provided.
Above there is a simple triple lancet.

SOUTH TRANSEPT AND CHAPELS

In the south-east corner of the south transept a staircase is
contained within the buttress, leading to triforium and
clerestory and, via the roof, to the central tower. In the
opposite corner of the south transept is a similar newel stair
leading to a small room now used as a store. This arrangement is repeated in the north transept, but the small room
here is very low and the upper portion houses the works
for the clock face. It contains some apparently original cupboards. It is possible to come out of these little rooms in
both transepts on to the sills of the windows, and it has
been suggested that they were used as watching chambers.

The triplets of shafts on either side of the main transept
windows are brought down to the usual water holding bases
standing on the bench in the south transept, but in the north
they end in corbels some eight feet from the ground. At first
sight they seem to have been cut off to make room for the
nineteenth century monument, but this is not so as the corbels
are ancient, although not the strip of carving carried across
between them. It would seem that an early easter sepulchre,
or something similar, stood here, but all traces are hidden
by the monument.

The transept aisle on the south-west is the only plain one
remaining : that on the south-east is divided to make two
chapels, St Calixtus nearer the crossing and St Martin of
Tours to the south. The dedication to St Calixtus is thought

to be a discreet reference by the Norman Bishop Reginald to
the Battle of Hastings, the commemoration being on the same
day. St Martin's dedication may derive from Bishop John of
Tours. The construction of these chapels is very interesting.
Wide arches have been cut deeply into the thick outside wall
to take the altars. The inside overhangs to form a rere arch.
Below, above the altars, are wide windows of the fourteenth
century. These are also much lower than the original lancets,
as may be seen from the string course outside. Between the
two chapels the normal thickness of wall persists for such
a short distance that it appears to stick out like a buttress,
but performs the essential purpose of supporting the ribs of
the vault arranged as one cell over each chapel. On it in St
Martin's chapel will be found the only trace of fresco painting
in the cathedral. It takes the form of imitation stone work.
This thinning of walls to take windows, and the use of intermediate buttresses to hold the vault was a device of late
perpendicular builders; the only difference here is that the
buttress is on the inside.

These two chapels are enclosed within a screen of Perpendicular date contemporary with that in the North Transept.
Here, however, entrance is given by two central doorways
from the transept, instead of from the Choir aisle. These are
now closed with wrought iron doors taken (probably in 1845)
from Beckington's tomb. At one time there were much higher
doors which covered the open tracery above, as may be seen
from the remaining hinges. No doubt care was taken about
1400 to cut off the nave from the choir right across the
church at this point, perhaps for security reasons. Built into
the space below the south window of St Martin's chapel and
so closing the Early English doorway to an outside vestry
(of which obvious traces remain) is the interesting tomb to
Canon Biconyll, † 1448. The effigy, of Dundry stone, lies
under a very flat four-centred arch with quatrefoils in the
spandrils. Above a course of vine leaf decoration is a row of
eleven tiny niches canopied with ogee finials and small
pinnacles. Apparently they never held statues. Above again
we find a row of paterae set in a hollow chamfer, the whole
being finished with a pointed cornice. The tomb chest below

the effigy has eleven blank panels resembling the niches above. All the work is characteristic of the period, if a little advanced for 1448. The canon is vested in choir habit : cassock, surplice, choir cope and almuce, and is tonsured.[28]

On the floor in front of the altar of this chapel is a most interesting memorial to Canon John Grene † 1409. This consists of a freestone slab with three rows of raised black-letter type in lead :

> *: Hic jacet: Johes grene coda*
> *canonic' hui' ecce qui obiit X die*
> *ms' Januar' a dni MCCCC N⁰.*

that is, 'Here lies John Grene, formerly canon of this church who died Jan. 10, 1409.' [29]

The adjoining chapel of St Calixtus housed for some years an enormous Gurney Stove curiously provided with the canopy from the Beckington Tomb in the choir. All was happily restored by Dean Robinson in 1920 and the east end panelled in sixteenth century style. There is one magnificent tomb built against the south wall containing the effigy of an unknown ecclesiastic, evidently a canon of the church. The hollow canopy of Doulting stone closely resembles that of Biconyll in the adjoining chapel, and the tomb seems to be of the same date as the screen separating the chapels. These facts reinforce the conjecture by St John Hope that the tomb is that of Thomas Boleyn, a Precentor † 1470. The panels in front are remarkably fine and are often reproduced. That on the left represents the Annunciation. Next there is the first of four shields all surmounted with a curious feather-like crown. They also show the 'fretty' part of the Boleyn coat of arms but not the rest, so that the attribution to Boleyn must remain very doubtful. The third panel contains in semi-relief one of the five weepers shown round the tomb, under elaborate canopies. These are beautiful little figures of canons of the period fully vested like the effigy above, and like Canon Biconyll next door. The extreme right-hand panel has a representation of the Holy Trinity, although without the Dove. The Father is shown with an elaborate crown and flowing hair. He holds a Tau crucifix which, here in this quiet corner, has been miraculously preserved from Puritan iconoclasts. The ends of the tomb also contain shields and weepers, that on the east badly damaged.[30]

The southern wall of the main south transept has been cut right back below the central lancet to house the beautiful tomb of Bishop William de Marchia, Treasurer of England 1290-5, and Bishop 1293–1302.[31] The original bench has been replaced by a long slab of Blue Lias and behind it rise three arches, cinqfoiled and triple cusped. They are surmounted by heavily crocketted ogees. We may note how the nod to ogee arches developed at Wells during the next twenty years, as they are found in the choir and Lady Chapel. The finials here are particularly large and the whole effect very rich. There is some castellation behind the arches, and inside a carefully constructed miniature vault of three cells. This has well moulded diagonal ribs and roof and transverse ribs, but no liernes : there are large bosses covered with foliage. The effigy of the bishop in Doulting stone is raised somewhat above bench level ; angels support the head and a dog the feet. The bishop is vested in amice, alb, maniple, tunicle, dalmatic, mitre and staff with sudery. This is a very early example, certainly the first at Wells, showing the tunicle on an episcopal effigy. On the back wall of the tomb are three figures, the central one having lost its head, of a bishop, vested as above, and with two censing angels at the sides.

At each end of the tomb are carved large heads, quite un- adorned, one male (bearded) and the other female. It can only be conjectured that these represent our Lord and our Lady. A row of male heads, no doubt by the same hand, are found along the main tomb slab. Dr Fryer thinks that this effigy was carved by the London School of statuaries.

We have seen that the space below the western lancet of the south wall is partly occupied by a staircase leading to a small room, long used as a vestry, which is really inside a main buttress. Here, however, a remarkable development has taken place. Access was originally provided by the stairs to the sill of the western lancet, but a passage way was after- wards cut through to the central window, i.e. to the roof of the Marcia tomb. The only explanation available is that relics were here displayed during the time attempts were being made to secure the canonization of the bishop.[32] The door of the staircase seems also to have been ornamented at this time with an ogee arch and also a band of frescoes was painted above it. Of this only one female head is now discernible.

East of the Marcia tomb, between it and the tower staircase, we find the canopy of a tomb of some unknown person. Although in some respects resembling the former, it is at least a quarter of a century later; indeed it may be as late as 1350. There is a large single arch of five trefoiled openings ending in an ogee and small finial. Surmounting this, and capped by a castellated parapet, is a row of perpendicular panels. Inside, at the back, are three niches which may have held staues. Above these the wall is pierced with openings to provide light, and the window sill of the main lancet has been cut down several feet for the purpose. Black paint is found in the window corresponding to that on the tomb, showing that it must be *in situ*.[33] The back wall of this tomb was plastered up until 1809 when Phelps the historian opened it up. At this time it was thought to belong to the Viscountess de Lisle, the inscription on whose monument 'in the transept,' had been recorded by Leland : *Hic jacet Joanna Vicecomitissa de Lisle, una filiarum et heredum Thomae Chedder, Armig. quae fuit uxor Joannis Vicecomitis de Lisle, filii et heredis Joannis Comitis Salopiae, et Margaretae ux' ejus, unius filiarum et heredum Ricardi Comitis Warwici, et Elizabeth uxoris ejus filiae et heredis Thomae de Berkley quae obiit XV die mensis Julii, Ann° D MCCCCLXIII*. So a new brass was made and erected here. Lady Lisle, however, died in 1464, which is an impossibly late date for this tomb, but the brass remains.[34] As we have seen, the second and third arches of the transept arcade open into chapels, the first, nearest the crossing, being the entrance to the choir aisle. Here we may notice the masterly planning of the crossing. The width of the choir aisle determines the width of its entrance, which is the first arch of the transept arcade. This distance between piers is naturally continued round the arcades of the transepts. From the west end of the nave there is thus a near perfect vista through the crossing to the choir aisle and chapels beyond. It must have been even better when the Early English vaulting went right through instead of being broken by the lierne work of the fourteenth century. All four transept chapels have what may be called the stump of a bench round them. The thick roll of the edge of the bench is attached directly to the wall and vaulting shafts are brought down on to it. The plinth also is set back to the main wall. In all four cases this roll has been cut off behind the altars and only the plinth remains. Whether this was to accommodate altars or later monuments and furniture, we do not know.

The dedications of the two chapels in the north transept were Corpus Christi, next the crossing, and Holy Cross.[35] Their construction appears to be identical with those on the south, except for window changes. The sills of these are original and much higher, since it was impossible to lower them in the fourteenth century owing to the roof of the undercroft passage outside. In contrast to the south, the Early English jambs remain, consisting of a single keeled shaft with floral capital and square abacus. There are the usual water-holding bases. The arch consists of a plain roll between two deep hollows and chamfers, and is so low as to be almost circular, although really two-centred. Adjoining the shafts is a thin space of blank walling, which is original, since it is bonded with the stones of the shafts. This somewhat lessens the width of window, which is now filled with glass and Decorated tracery. The width however is eight feet, which is quite out of proportion for a lancet. We can only postulate, therefore, a greater space of blank wall in Early English days, with a lancet or possibly a triplet in the middle.

Some suggestion has been made that these altar windows give the pattern for those in the choir aisles, all of which have been changed. This however cannot be so, as the thickness of wall is quite different. It seems likely that the choir aisle windows resembled those of the nave.

In both transepts, a few shafts, not on the piers, are found without necking. There seems no reason for this, but it may be an indication of early work. Part of the base of the respond at the entrance to St Martin's chapel has been altered to form two plain steps to support some stone erection or perhaps a seat for a guardian.

CAPITALS—THE DEVELOPING EARLY ENGLISH STYLE

The capitals of the eastern arcades of the transepts have only foliage carving, with the exception of one bird. The necks of these capitals however are lowered in gradation going north and south, thus giving a deeper capital. It was evidently decided that they were too short in the choir and the change was made gradually. This device is so effective that very few people notice it.

The capitals on the west are profusely decorated with figures, more so than any others in the cathedral.

It is rather difficult to account for this sudden change in the same transept, especially as it takes place laterally. Perhaps the eastern range was built before the western, although this does not seem likely. It may be that these usually amusing figures were not considered suitable for chapels but might be allowed at the back in the more utilitarian aisle.

Numbering the capitals from the cloister door, we find on the first (respond) two heads, male and female and a grotesque mask. The second is the most elaborate in the cathedral, and has the story of the vineyard robbers. Firstly we see a bearded thief about to cut a bunch of grapes with a sickle. He looks round as if fearing discovery, while a boy holds a basket containing more grapes.

We next see the farmer's man with a crooked stick pointing out the thieves to his master. Thirdly, the farmer has caught the elder thief by his ear, and lastly, is hitting him over the head with a fork. The third capital is known as the 'toothache capital' from the fine head of a man with his finger in his mouth. Other single figures on this capital are : a woman extracting a thorn from her foot : a head with long tongue : a man's head : a woman's head with long plaited hair : a cobbler at work : a baboon. The next capital is the respond at the crossing and this has one of the few inscriptions, which are all in Lombardic capitals on bannerets held by figures. Thus a man here has 'ELIAS : P.' There are three other male heads on the capital, one with curly hair and one with its tongue out, and, between them, a devil with ass's ears.

NORTH TRANSEPT AND CHAPELS

Crossing over to the other respond in the north transept we
find a head with a flat hat. The third capital is one of those
framing the clock. It has, firstly, a figure of a man holding
a banneret inscribed, '. . . ARON.' The beginning of the
wording is cut off by the woodwork of the clock, but in fact
the back portion of the capital was destroyed when the clock
was erected. No doubt it contained the other 'A.' Next is a
fine seated figure of Moses with his right hand raised in
blessing, and holding the tablets on his left knee. These are
plainly inscribed 'LEGE DEI.' On the window side of this
capital is a mysterious figure of a man seated and writing out
a banneret with a pen. He has got as far as the three letters
'AIA . . .' We next come to the respond against the north
wall which has the figure of a man with a goose, partly in
a box, over his shoulder : a face with mouth awry : two heads.
Inside, in the canon's vestry is found a man holding a blank
banneret. There is also here a large cupboard or cloakroom
contained in the base of the transept buttress and below the
small 'watching room' already mentioned. Over the doorway
we see a charming little statue of a woman about two feet
high under a plain canopy. She is dressed in a single garment
from neck to foot, girdled at the waist and her head is
wrapped. Under was an inscription, probably her name, which
most unfortunately has been destroyed, except the last two
letters 'L E' and the usual triple stop. There is every indication that this statue is contemporary with the building of the
transept, *c.* 1190. It is the only one in the church which has
survived at this level, and no doubt owes its preservation to
the fact that it was inside this room. The statue may possibly
represent St Sidwell, who was martyred at Exeter in 740.[36]

The stone screen now separating the Chapels of Corpus
Christi (south) and Holy Cross (north), from the north transept
dates at *c.* 1400. Previously, entrance to the Chapter House
stairway was gained indiscriminately from the transept. We
may enquire whether there was in fact an entrance to the
church here before the Chapter House was built. In spite of

such an assumption by Dean Robinson, this seems unlikely. The door is very small and is exactly like its fellow in the south transept (St Martin's Chapel), which manifestly led to a vestry. Be that as it may, the new screenwork now made entrance to the Chapter House difficult, more especially since two large 'altar' tombs separated the chapels which had to be traversed. The slabs of these tombs were sunk to floor level during the restorations of 1840–60, and are still in place. Before this was done, however, there was little space to pass between them and the transept piers on the way to the Chapter House. To get over the difficulty the piers were slightly modified. That on the north has had the Early English base removed and a much shallower one of the fifteenth century substituted. The same sort of thing has happened to the southern pier, but in a more interesting way. The inner face of this pier formerly had a single shaft resting on a broad, water-holding base of Early English date. The large broad stone has probably been removed and re-inserted some ten feet up from the ground where it now forms a corbel supporting the same shaft. The water-holding base remains, but the great mass of stone has been carved back into the beautiful lizard-like animal we now see. Dean Robinson investigated the vault below the southern tombstone, and found that the body was sewn up in leather as if brought from a distance. There was the usual mortuary chalice and paten of lead. It seems likely that this was the tomb of one William de Wellington as there is a reference to his chantry, 'at the altar of Corpus Christi under the belfry of the church of Wells,' in 1378. It is interesting to note that this dedication was thus retained after a new chapel of Corpus Christi (II) was built farther east in 1330. The chapel now contains the elaborate Jacobean tomb of Bishop Still, 1592–1607, removed here from the south side of the High Altar. In this bishop's time the lead mines on the episcopal estate near Wells were very profitable, or as Fuller quaintly puts it, 'In his days God opened the bosome of the earth, Mendip Hills affording great store of Lead.' So Wells enjoys this fine monument, the only one of its kind in the cathedral, and £500 given to the Bubwith Almshouse.

Memoriae sacrum
Joanni Still Episcopo Bathoniensi et Wellensi, Sacrae
Theologiae Doctori Acerrimo Christianae Veritatis
propugnatori non minus vitae integritate quam varia
Doctrina claro qui cum Domino Diu vigilasset in
Christo spe certa resurgendi obdormivit die XXVI
Februarii MDCVII
Vixit annos LXIIII sedit episcopus XVI
Nathaniel Still filius primogenitus optimo patri
Moerens pietatis ergo posuit.

The arms shown on the tomb are those of the See and of
Still : *Sa . , gutte de l'eau and three roses arg.*

Occupying a similar eastern position in the next chapel is
a large marble monument to Bishop Kidder. This prelate
eventually succeeded the saintly Bishop Ken who had been
deprived, and was killed with his wife at the palace during
the night of 26/27 November, 1703, by the fall of a stack
of chimneys during the great storm which then ravaged the
west country. Jewers gives a transcription of the very long
epitaph. The tomb was removed from the north side of the
High Altar, where it had been erected by the daughter of
the bishop, who is seen gazing at two urns representing the
remains of her parents.[37]

On the north wall of the Chapel of the Holy Cross is the
interesting tomb of Bishop Thomas Cornish. He had been
Prebendary, Chancellor, Succentor, and Precentor of the
cathedral, Rector of Lambrook, and Vicar of St Cuthbert's,
Wells, Chew Magna and Wedmore. For some years before
his death in 1513 he had done most of the work in the diocese
as suffragan bishop. As was the custom in those days he took
his title from the Greek island of Tenos, *in partibus infidelium.*
The bishops of the diocese were largely absent on affairs of
state, and, as the registers show, did not even conduct their
own ordinations.[38] The tomb has a canopy of very conventional perpendicular work of the time, the ceiling of which
however is curious in that there is carved upon its perfectly
flat surface a representation in low relief of a fan vault. On
the front of the chest are three shields (1) a T with a wheat-

sheaf, (2) *On a chev. betw. three birds' heads erased a mitre, Cornish,* (3) a C with another wheatsheaf. At the west end are the usual arms of the See, the saltire being plain without any partition lines. Between the mouldings of the Purbeck marble slab covering the chest is a strip of brass partly destroyed and now reading : *Obiit supradictus dñs Thomas Epūs tercio die mensis Julii anno MCCCCCXIII Cujus Anime P(ropitietur Deus A) M.E.N*. On the west wall at the back of the tomb is the matrix of a pictorial brass showing a figure of the bishop kneeling, with a prayer coming from his mouth. The space between the tomb and the eastern wall of the chapel is now filled with plain masonry, and on the face of this overlooking the slab is a draped figure with naked chest and feet, carved in freestone, coming out of a square headed opening set in a larger arch. Below is a kneeling figure holding a staff. Both have been mutilated, but it is almost certain that they represent the Resurrection of our Lord, with Bishop Cornish kneeling before Him. Such carvings are frequently found on tombs which were intended to be used as Eastern Sepulchres. The Host was housed in a portable wooden casket placed on the top of the tomb. However, as we shall see later, another tomb in Corpus Christi Chapel (II) lays claim to this distinction : perhaps both were used at different times.

THE ASTRONOMICAL CLOCK[39]

Two vestries now occupy the west aisle of the north transept, corresponding with the chapels of the Holy Cross and Corpus Christi on the eastern side. The southern one, entered from the nave through a perpendicular screen, is used by the Vicars Choral. Panelling of the same date, *c.* 1400, closes the arches to the transept, forming walls to the vestries. The space above the panelling of the Vicars' vestry is occupied by the main face of the magnificent medieval clock. From the works situated behind and above this face, power is transmitted by wires and levers to the face outside the transept, the knights above it, the 'Jack Blandiver' figure seated in the transept triforium, and the great hour bell in the central tower. Just as the documents at Wells provide few building dates, so they are silent as to the origin of the clock. It is known that clocks were made at Glastonbury Abbey and particularly by the monk Peter Lightfoot, and it is a reasonable assumption, although nothing more, that the Wells clock came from those workshops. The story that it was removed from the abbey at the Reformation is most unlikely to be true.

The earliest payment for the keeper of a clock was for the year 1392-3 : *In stipendium custodientis la clokk 10/- per annum*. According to some experts this date is rather late, and the clock may have been installed somewhat earlier in the century. On the other hand this main face fits perfectly with the stone screen below, which can also be dated at *c*. 1400. The face is of wood, square, with a circle inside. The four blank corners so formed are filled with paintings of angels, although there is no indication that they represent the four cardinal winds. The outer circular rim is divided into twenty-four parts, each hour being indicated by Roman numerals in two lots of twelve. These are on attached wooden discs.[40] A large multi-pointed star moves round to indicate the hour. A second rim inside the outer one shows the minutes. Every fifth is indicated on a square tablet, 5, 10, etc., the intermediate minutes being shown by plain strokes on rectangular tablets. The third and inner disc shows the thirty days of the lunar month, also painted on square tablets.[41] A trident indicator is fixed to a flat disc of wood, the whole of which moves round. Between indicator and axis is a circular window and, as the disc revolves, parts of the moon, painted behind, are revealed. These correspond to the numbers shown by the indicator, thus at fourteen days the full moon appears and so on. Round this circular moon window are painted the words *Sphericus archetypum globus hic monstrat microcosmum*[42] in lettering which is probably original (*c*. 1400). Also painted on the central disc is a representation of the Goddess Phoebe (for the Moon), with the text *Sic peragrat Phoebe*. This lettering is later and probably dates from the time of the repainting of the minute and date numbers. Above this great clock face a semi-octagonal tray has in its centre a wooden turret, battlemented and panelled in early Perpendicu-

lar style. Round the turret takes place the famous little
tourney every visitor to Wells remembers at the ¼ hour in
summer and ½ hour in winter.

The life size figure seated under a sentry box in the
triforium above the clock strikes the quarters by raising its
feet from bells beneath the seat. He strikes the bell suspended
in front of him. It seems impossible to guess at the date of
this oaken figure. His costume is so plain as to be ageless, and
we have to remember that repainting, and possibly renewal
of the legs, has undoubtedly taken place. The design of the
box is just plain perpendicular of the fourteenth or fifteenth
centuries. It is quite possible that the whole arrangement is
as old as the clock. Even the name 'Jack Blandiver' is
mysterious.

The exterior face of the clock, fixed to the front of the
western buttress of the north transept, is very satisfying in
spite of the mixture of styles. As inside, the four corners are
filled with symbolic figures, here in low relief, and of the four
evangelists, Winged Man, Lion, Ox and Eagle for SS
Matthew, Mark, Luke and John. Each holds a banneret with
his name in Latin. The plain dial belongs to the early part
of the last century. It would originally have been divided
into the twenty-four hours. Above the face are two wooden
knightly figures in armour which turn and strike the quarters
on bells suspended above them. From their dress they can
be accurately dated at 1485–90, and so are later than the
original clock. The remaining function of the works is to
strike the hour bell, mounted in a turret of the central tower.
Except for the escapement which is of the Galileo type invented in the seventeenth century, the original works func-
tioned until the nineteenth century, when they were unfortunately sent to the Science Museum. Here they were put
in order and still run perfectly. The modern works have
received much expensive attention and renewal since 1883.

THE FONT

The circular font has been so badly treated that it is
difficult to date. The bowl, or rather cylinder of a single
block of Doulting stone stands on a plain platform and base.

An arcade of eight arches has been cut round it. These are slightly pointed inside and circular outside.

In the tympana are carved what appear to be bunches of three flowers. The whole however has at some time been cut right back by chiselling in some tidying-up operation. In particular the capitals and bases of the arcade are now quite plain and have given rise to conjectures of a Saxon origin which does not seem likely. Before it was scraped the font was covered with a dark red paint still visible in the declivities.

In seven of the eight arches there are signs of some circular medallion-like decoration having been removed. This would indicate a date of the mid-thirteenth century. The oaken cover is good Jacobean work.

The font is so well placed and proportioned that it seems likely that it was designed for its present position and is not older than the church.

The present rood was erected in the time of Dean Robinson on the inverted arch towards the nave. It does however rest on the holes of the old sockets, the stump of the old cross being preserved in the Library.

CHAPTER III

THE EARLY ENGLISH CHURCH
(THE NAVE)

THE interior of the nave at Wells has been rightly called the first example of the purely Early English style. Save perhaps for the squared abacus of the piers, hardly a trace of Norman influence remains. In this it differs considerably from contemporary work at Glastonbury.

Building must have proceeded westwards from the crossing, after the completion of the short choir of three bays and the north and south transepts. Since progress was at first rapid, we may suppose that it had proceeded as far as the nave by 1200, and that the first portion of this had been completed by the time that Bishop Reginald's successor Savaric died in 1205. There was then a pause of some years until Jocelin of Wells finished the nave, so that the whole might be consecrated in 1239. The nave piers are similar to those in the earlier transepts but slightly farther apart. An important change was made at triforium level. Here three arched openings were placed in each bay instead of two, and the row made continuous right down the church. This means that the shafts supporting the corbels from which the high vault springs have to be cut short and not brought down to pier level. A similar continuity of triforium had been achieved on the north and south walls of the transepts where there were no vault corbels to be considered, and the idea may then have been adopted for the whole nave. Be that as it may, this continuous line of small openings makes the nave appear much longer than it really is. The large triforium chamber behind the arches should perhaps be called a tribune, although there are no windows to light it. The chief feature inside is the massive flying buttresses which convey the thrust of the high vault to the buttresses supporting the aisle walls. The first bay of the nave was considerably altered when the central tower began to collapse in 1338. Thus the main arches have been rebuilt and their moulding is of the fourteenth century. The inner triplet shafts of the piers have also been renewed with caps and bases of the later date. Two triforium arches on each side have been filled in to give greater strength and above, at clerestory level, may be seen filling and traces of buttresses built to support the tower.

It should be noted that the ritual choir extended westwards at this time as far as the first pier of the nave. Here was a screen right across nave and aisles, with doors leading eastwards into the aisles. There are obvious signs of the attachment of this screen, probably of wood, to the piers, etc. The stalls of the clergy extended under the crossing eastwards to the present stone choir screen or pulpitum, which did not then exist, and the three-bay eastern arm of the church was an open space kept clear for ceremonial purposes.

Although the main piers seem to be a mass of shafting, the construction is really quite simple. The plan is a square with smaller squares cut out of each corner. The eight new corners thus produced are clearly visible. On each face of the original square is a plain triplet of shafts, with 'water-holding' bases; similar triplets, the centre one being keeled, are placed in spaces provided by the removal of the corners. The capitals have conventional foliage. Some figures are incorporated, but not as many as in the transepts. All are necked, but the necks are lower than in the older work of the choir. Above is the squared abacus usually only found in twelfth century work. In some of the earlier piers the upper edge of this is not chamfered. Towards the aisles the outer triplet holds the ribs of the aisle vault. The diagonal or corner triplets on this side support an order of the pier arch. The pair of inner triplets take another (the first) order. On the front side of the main pier we would expect the facing triplets to hold the ribs supporting the high vault. Instead they support an extra order of the arch, which thus has three orders towards the nave, and two towards the aisles. The reason probably was that the earlier builders did not like to risk a two order arch and the thinner wall which it would support.

In the centre of the nave floor, just west of the chantries, is a small stone marked INA REX. This was placed here in 1917 on the supposed site of a large memorial known at one time to exist to the founder of the church, King Ina of the West Saxons who, however, was buried in Rome where he had become a monk. Under this stone was found a coffin, made for an ecclesiastic since a chalice space was provided. This may well have belonged to Bishop Burnell † 1292, the first bishop to be buried in the nave. The cathedral has two beautiful relics which were dug up, unfortunately at a time when records were not kept, about 1800. It seems likely that they came from this coffin. The first is a brass pastoral staff, and the second a leaden crucifix, painted and gilded.

THE BREAK IN BUILDING

Proceeding westwards from this stone there is little of special interest, until we come to the 'break,' probably marking the place where Bishop Jocelin took over the work of building. He succeeded in 1206, but it is unlikely that he commenced building until later, as he was abroad under interdict. So many and definite are the changes to be observed at the break that work probably ceased for at least fifteen years. In order to follow these changes it is necessary to realize that, owing to the thrust of the arcades, a building of this kind cannot be left with a vertical end as a plain wall might be. Thus the older portion proceeded farther westwards at ground level than higher up, and so the line of demarcation is inclined towards the east. A glance at the fourth capitals from the *west* end will show them to be the last of the old work. The third pair have more elaborate and undercut foliage. From the old pier 4, the line of demarcation slopes so that it reaches the high vault two bays nearer the crossing. Thus there are six bays of old work at ground level and only four at the vault. In the aisles we find the break in the walls to be in the centre of the fourth bay on the north, and at the beginning of that bay on the south. These latter breaks may be easily observed, as the courses of ashlar in the walls change considerably. The vaults of the aisles of the old work extended one bay westward of the high vault. A very jagged end must thus have been left, and this may account for Jocelin's complaint that he found the church in a 'ruinous' condition when he arrived. The following are the principal changes which took place at the break :

(1) *High Vault*. Many more stones (voussoirs) are used to make up the ribs in the older portion.

(2) *Main Arcade*. The plain ashlar masonry over the arches, but below the triforium, has several more courses in the older work, that is, smaller stones are used. We might conclude that improved techniques allowed the transport and handling of larger stones in the new part were it not for the fact that we find the large size of stone used in the choir for the earliest work of all.

(3) *Tooling of stones*. Norman builders obtained plain surfaces with an axe, striking diagonally, and leaving a mark sometimes called cross hatching. Later this was done with a chisel, leaving vertical hatching. At Wells it is very clear that the old practice obtained up to the break, and the new one afterwards.

(4) *Aisle vaulting*. The diagonal ribs of the later section have a fillet.

(5) *Hood Moulding*. This is stopped over the main piers with small heads up to the break, but not afterwards.

(6) *Triforium*. There are medallions of foliage carving in the spandrils of the arches right down the nave. Up to the break, however, these are more deeply cut into the wall and the edges are chamfered.

(7) *Keystones*. In the new section the pier arches are built up on each side to meet exactly in the centre where there is a vertical joint. In the older part the builders adopted the much sounder policy of having a keystone at the head of each arch, so that the joint is avoided.

The following innovations are found in the western part of the nave, although there is no sudden change at the break :

(1) Bases of pier shafts. Several of these have a double or more elaborate fillet. (It is necessary to disregard an unfortunate restoration near the pulpit.)

(2) The principle of Tas de Charge, or the use of horizontally laid overlapping stones is adopted to begin some of the vaulting of the aisles.

Two details in the middle nave should be noticed. There

is a gallery contrived below a clerestory window on the south side. These are found in a number of larger churches, notably Exeter cathedral. No better explanation seems available than that they were used by musicians for some rather indeterminate liturgical purpose. This one was erected about 1450.

Two large heads, one of a bishop and one of a king, appear in the spandrils of the main south arcade near the west end. Heads of king and bishop are very often found outside the west doors of parish churches, usually as stops to the drip mould. They are probably no more than reminders to worshippers of their duties to both Church and State. The arms of the king and bishop were later substituted, and this was probably the origin of the royal arms which became a feature in churches in post-Reformation days. The custom of erecting the heads, however, did not begin until long after the west front of the cathedral was built. It would then have been difficult to find a place for them amidst the mass of carving, and so they were put inside.

INSIDE THE WEST END

We now come to consider the interior of the west front. We do not know what sort of building Bishop Reginald intended, but it is abundantly clear that Bishop Jocelin wished primarily to erect a great statuary screen, only incidentally providing an abutment for the nave arcades. This he achieved principally by placing the bases of the western towers outside the nave aisles to north and south. Inside, spaces are thus obtained, under the towers entered from the nave, which very much resemble the porticoes of Saxon churches. This arrangement is unique in England although it would seem that the Norman Priory of St Botolph, Colchester, now destroyed, adopted it, with two chapels attached to the aisles. At Ripon the two towers in the early church stood outside an aisleless nave, and at Peterborough there is an obvious western transept, although the towers stop the ends of the aisles. Some writers have considered that this plan at Wells was an old one based on the Saxon tradition and re-adopted by Jocelin. Under the north-west tower is the strikingly beautiful chapel of the Holy Cross, now somewhat degraded from its original purpose, to serve both as a consistory court and a choir boys' vestry. It would seem from a statement by Leland that this was the chantry chapel of John Storthwaite, Chancellor. *Joannes Storthwaite Cancellar Wellensis executor Bubbewith Episcopi Bathon. fecit Capellam et Cantarium in Boreal. parte primi transepti.* It is interesting to notice that he calls this part of the church the first transept.

Here we see the mature Early English style at its best, and meet for the first time with the insets of Blue Lias for shafts and abaci, used so much at Wells and Glastonbury for the next three-quarters of a century until, for a time, those of the more expensive Purbeck Marble took their place. In this chapel a wooden floor has been inserted at bench level. It seems to have been the practice at Wells to continue the bench right round the chapel, which must have interfered with the erection of the altar. There are signs of a reredos having been fixed to the east wall. Here we find also an interesting but simple piscina contrived amidst the shafts of the entrance doorway. This is the only Early English specimen left in the cathedral and, very curiously, it has only one drain. It must have been put here quite early in the thirteenth century since double piscinas were universally used as the century advanced.

The space under the south-west tower, similar to the Holy Cross chapel, forms the entrance to the west walk of the cloisters. It has been suggested that it was also the main entrance for the lay people from the west, and that they did not use the doors on the west front, then opening on to the cemetery. There is a curiously plain and cumbersome porch leading from the green into the third bay of the cloisters, and thence into this space.

Is there another 'break' between the west front and the nave? There is most certainly one of style of perhaps half a century. Even the capital of the arcade respond is in two parts, one with a round and the other with square abacus, and the end wall is ornamented with Lias shafts and other work typical of the third decade of the century. Some of these shafts, the larger ones, were rebuilt with Draycott conglomerate, three before 1824.

We can see, by the small doorways, another curious and ungainly device to stretch the front by a mere three feet to add to the statuary screen. The windows at the ends of the aisles, since they fit into the vaults, must pierce the front at fixed places. One would expect them to do so centrally over the little doors and centrally between the buttresses outside. At first sight this appears to be the case, but if we look again we can see that the front has been stretched away, as it were, from these fixed points to gain about eighteen inches on each side. The architect has thus made the bays slightly asymmetric, perhaps hoping that this would not be noticed. Inside, the design has been so distorted that the Lias shafts supporting the vaults have had to be omitted to the north and south.

Although there is such a difference in style, we find no sign of a break in construction. As we have seen, it would have been impossible to stop building vertically at the end of the nave without putting up the front to take the thrust of the arcades. The reasonable conclusion seems to be that there was continuous building of the western portion of the nave and the front from 1220 to 1239, when the whole was consecrated, the newer part of the nave being made deliberately archaic to match the work of c. 1200.

It has been suggested recently that the west front was not structurally completed until 1260 but, in fact, all the work outside, with the exception of a single row of deeply undercut carving over the main door, corresponds with what is found elsewhere belonging to the third decade of the century, though some or all of the statues *may* have been added later.

The triple lancet of the great west window was designed to include Lias columns inside. The heavy bases and capitals are in position, and portions of the midway rings also remain built into the wall. It would seem that these columns may have been removed at some later date, when, as happened outside, they gave trouble by splitting. The effect of removal is to let in more light; also the plain lancets match the older nave much better than an arcade would have done. Possibly the builders did not pursue their original intention and the latter was never made.

There is a walk across the front of the window, thus linking both sections of the triforium. Its balustrading was plainly added in perpendicular times. Under this is a long chamber, about the width of the window and very narrow, built into the thickness of the wall. It has small circular openings behind the carvings on the west front, and therefore hardly visible. This may have been a gallery for singers, so that the sound would go out over the green as processions approached the west door. In many Somerset churches this provision for a singers' gallery has been made inside the porches and one, in wood, is still *in situ* at Weston-in-Gordano.

It will be noticed that, with the exception of the western triplet, all the windows of the nave have had early Perpendicular tracery inserted into the lancets. As one of this type in the south transept has been blocked by the cloister library erected *c.* 1425, the work was probably done before this date.

THE NORTH PORCH

This beautiful entrance to the nave formed the *porta magna* for the clergy, since the houses of the *quinque personae* were ranged near it, and there was also a road opposite, now closed, leading to the Back, or North Liberty. Various dates have been assigned to the porch, from 1174 to 1230.

The hatching evidence is confusing. Outside the stone is weathered and inside there has, in the past, been much white-washing. When this is cleared by scraping, a kind of pseudo-vertical hatching is revealed, as Dean Robinson observed in the nave. Cross hatching is however certainly present in places. This confusion could be resolved if we assumed that the porch was built, together with the south doorways and central tower lantern, during the 'gap.' There remains the objection that the builders would be more likely to push forward with the nave, rather than leave it and attend to these details.

There is no sign whatever of a pause in construction. The courses of masonry follow round perfectly from the nave into the porch. The very nature of the stone is similar, it being porous with a considerable amount of the red colour of iron. The shafts on the outer doorway and of the work inside are ringed. Such annulation is only found at Wells in three places : here, in the south doorways, and in the lantern of the central tower. This must exclude the possibility of a twelfth century date. More formidable still is the fact that all the vault ribs are filleted, different from the aisle just inside, and like the later section of the nave. The inner doorway has a distinctly Norman appearance with a zig-zag moulding. Its Trumeau, or stone division, has clearly been inserted in the fifteenth century. This, on the other hand, is strong evidence for a very *early* thirteenth century date, since the great west door has one. We are here in the pre-Trumeau or nearly Norman era. In the capitals of this doorway are figures on either side. That on the west is of a bishop in chasuble and mitre. An ecclesiastic on the east carries a banneret which is much broken and reads : *INT : IN G . . . VD . . . II . . . TUI,* that is *INTRA: IN: GAUDIUM: DOMINI: TUI.*

It would be difficult to imagine anything more lovely than the blank arcading of the interior of the porch. It rests on a bench which is curious in that the moulding is much more elaborate than is found elsewhere in the cathedral until the fifteenth century. It may have been cut later. Standing on the bench are large shafts, each having two rings and a spurred base. The latter is found nowhere else in the building. The shafts support the usual E.E. vault dividing the porch into two bays. The capitals are in some cases much undercut.

At the back of the bench the wall is hollowed as if to provide seats, four to a bay. In the spandrils of these arched hollows there is a variety of fine carving, some of it with figures. Each set of four seats supports these arches deeply cut into the wall and provided with a profusion of annulated shafts with good foliage capitals. Everywhere is the square abacus and no lias insets. So we are again forced, almost against our will, to assign a fairly early date to the porch. Above, just below the vault, are plain blank windows, the moulding in front running together to form Y arches, like later tracery.

The great outer arch of three orders bears definite traces of Norman influence. It is supported on each side by eight

annulated shafts with foliated capitals. Those on the north
contain the story of the martyrdom of St Edmund. In spite
of weathering over seven hundred years these small figures
remain some of the finest in the cathedral. Starting from the
outside we see the king, crowned but stripped to the waist,
pierced with arrows from bowmen on each side. Next we see
the beheading, the king still crowned with head bowed to
the front and a warrior standing by with raised arm. There
follows a scene, either of the warrior giving the head to a
wild beast or receiving it from the beast, according to the
tradition of its recovery. The next and last scene has been
woefully mutilated by being cut through to take the modern
outer doors. All that can be distinguished are two heads,
probably of soldiers, and the wild beast, this time moving
away. He may have left the head with them.

The staircase to the parvise or upper room begins in the
nave aisle, just east of the porch. It is contrived mostly in
the thickness of the wall, and originally penetrated through
the floor some six feet or so into the room. From the head
a door led into the parvise at floor level. This arrangement
is commonly found with newel staircases, it may be to prevent
people falling down the well, for greater security, or to keep
out the draught.

Over the whole of the floor of this chamber is a layer of
gypsum plaster, and this is covered with a maze of lines,
mostly straight, and criss-crossing in every direction. There
are a few arcs of large circles and a number of small complete circles. The writer suggests that this room was used
for cutting sheets of lead for roofing, probably at the Restoration in 1662 when large sums were spent on lead for this
purpose. The room is ideally situated to give easy access
to the roofs, although it would have been virtually impossible
to get sheets of lead up the newel stairs. For this reason we
find that the head of the medieval staircase has been rudely
destroyed because it closed access to the triforium and thence
to the roofs. This destruction has made it possible for sheets
of lead to be hauled from the nave floor and straight into
the room for cutting. Similar lines are found elsewhere in
the cathedral where lead might be cut for roofs, or possibly

to repair windows. It has been suggested that we have in the parvise a medieval architects' drawing floor, but this seems unlikely for a variety of reasons, the chief being that none of the 'drawings' can be recognised as parts of the cathedral building.

Outside, the North Porch so strongly resembles its near neighbour the North Transept, that it is difficult indeed to believe that it was not erected within the same decade. The corner buttresses like those on the transept aisles are carried straight up in one stage to roof level, and have identical pinnacles and caps except they are slightly smaller. The buttresses have at their corners attached shafts with leaf capitals. The gable end of the porch has an arcade of six arches with simple rolls from base to apex. The two centre arches are larger and of the same height. Their inner slopes are brought on to a common square abacus and capital, the shaft of which ends abruptly on a corbel. This would leave below a large space of blank wall, but in it has been contrived a charming triplet of lancet windows lighting the parvise room. Blank spaces above are filled with groups of foliage carving exactly as on the transept. The whole of this composition rests on a string course which is really a continuation of the corbel table brought round from the sides. The tympanum of the great arch of the door below this string course is relieved by two fairly large panels of carving representing two wild beasts one on each side. Speculations as to their identity are legion : cockatrice, lion, etc.

THE CROSSING AND LANTERN TOWER

The arches of the crossing, apart from the fourteenth century supports, are simple enough in construction and need not detain us. The lantern, however, now obscured by a late fan vault, has many points of interest.

Outside, Early English building clearly reaches to the apex of the roof, the blank walls being covered with a simple rolled arcade as on the transepts. Inside, the first stage consists of an impressive arcade of sixteen arches, four on each side, and must have looked well when open to the floor of the church. Some of the rolls of the arches come right down to the base and others rest on circular caps, three to each pier. Enclosed within these arches are sixteen smaller ones without capitals. Eight of these at the corners lead to the respective lofts of transepts, choir and nave. The others are blank. A bold string course crowns the whole stage. Above, a portion only of the second stage was completed by the Early English builders. This is of twelve arches, three on each side. They are deep enough to allow space for a passage right round the tower.

The first half of the piers was built at this time, the height corresponding to the roof apex. As the inner shafts of the piers are annulated, we can double the distance of ring from floor and so find the height of the proposed capitals of the arcade. This would bring them about a third higher than at present. The change in masonry on the plain surfaces between the arches is obvious enough just above the rings. This second arcade was completed at the present lower height, when the tower was built about 1320. Meanwhile in the intervening century there must have been a temporary roof, probably of wood. No trace of it remains. The chief point of interest about this lantern is that it is all built of cross hatched stones, and yet has the first circular, as opposed to square, abacus and the first rings. The Revd G. A. A. Wright, who made an extensive study of masons' marks throughout the cathedral finds all these in the tower to be after 1206.[43] It is clear that the lantern was built before work was resumed for the second part of the nave, when vertical hatching appears. On the other hand the capitals, being ringed, are later in style.

We can also add to this group of buildings the first few courses of the undercroft. Possibly this work was the cause of the break in the nave : it may have been decided to consolidate the previous work, with some refinements, before proceeding with the nave. This finding of cross hatching with rings and a circular abacus underlines the fact that much of the nave, perhaps before the gap, was built in an old-fashioned style in order to match what had gone before.

In writing of the great earthquake of 1248, Matthew Paris reports the fall of the *Tholus* on Wells Cathedral. Dean

Robinson has examined the various uses of this word and they are obscure.[44] The primary meaning seems to be a dome, but medieval writers extended this to any ornament crowning a building. Paris says : *Tholus quoque lapideus, magnae quantitatis et ponderis, qui per diligentiam caementariorum in summitate ecclesiae de Welles ad decorem ponebatur, raptus de loco suo, non sine dampno fabricae culminis cecedit, et cum ab alto rueret, tumultum reddens horribilem, audientibus timorem incussit non minimum.* He goes on to speak of further damage : *caminorum, propugnaculorum et columpnarum capitella et summitates.* Dr Robinson assumes the *tholus lapideus* to be some small decoration, but this hardly seems to justify *lapideus magnae quantitatis et ponderis.* Freeman considers that the vault of the church is meant, and that this accounts for the break in the nave, while repairs were in progress. Church minimizes the whole affair for the very good reasons that the records of the Chapter are silent and no damage to the twelfth century capitals or piers is evident. Also Bishop Bytton I, who recounts the story, was in Rome at the time. Wright, however, considers that the whole of the lantern of the central tower fell in 1248. In this case it must have been rebuilt with the same stones, since they are cross hatched and certainly earlier than 1248. The unfinished state of the second stage of the lantern may be the result of some fall but it seems more likely that it was never completed or was taken down to roof level by the fourteenth century builders.

NAVE CAPITALS—FLOWERING AND DECLINE OF THE STYLE

Although the capitals of the nave have fewer figures in them than those in the transepts, many are interesting. Numbering from the crossing on the south, the second has several figures : a man attacked by a lion : a lyre bird : an eagle with its head broken off. Inside the chantry, an owl : a figure in a gown holding a scroll.

The third capital on the south has two birds with long twisted necks and human heads, one in a jester's cap. The fifth has two fighting dragons and one has thrust a spear down the throat of the other. There are on the same capital two small devil heads. The sixth has a single male head, but the others on this side, belonging to the second phase of nave building, have foliage only.

On the north side of the nave the first capital of the arcade adjoining the cresting of the Bubwith chantry has an interesting figure of a packman carrying wares, including apparently a string of beads. Three additional figures were discovered on this capital in 1961. They had remained hidden by the cresting of the Bubwith Chantry below. Following on from the packman, the first is a seated figure, man or maybe woman, combing wool which is wound round a knee. The second is of a woman (decapitated) sitting and spinning, the usual distaff between her legs. The third is of the prophet Daniel, standing and holding a banneret with his name in Lombardic letters. The second capital has a fox carrying a goose, and a farmer with a sickle in pursuit : three birds preening themselves. Inside the chantry on the same capital is a spoonbill swallowing a frog : a devil with a long curly tail holding up a fish in his left hand and a billhook in his right.

The fourth capital by the north door has a bird with a crowned human head holding a sceptre : a ram with curly fleece : two human headed birds : a lion licking itself : dragons and birds including grotesque heads of pig and dog. The other capital by the north door has two beasts facing each other and some dragons, one wearing a coronet.

The next capital going west, that is Number 6, has two birds preening themselves : goats' and rams' heads : a grotesque head and two birds eating foliage. Number 7 has doves and other birds. Number 8 has a female head coming out of a kind of sheath. This capital and one on the south side clearly shows its derivation from the well defined trumpet type usually considered as late Norman.

The last capital and the respond show only foliage, deeply undercut. We should notice the remarkable change of style in the respond itself : the third order of the arch is brought down on to a circular piece of abacus with capital on a single 'marble' shaft. This adjoins the west front, all built, inside and out, in the mature Early English of the thirteenth century. The transition has been cleverly and carefully made. The last piece of capital has been much damaged but its carving is very simple and archaic, almost in the Classical Ionic style.

Only three monuments of importance remain in the nave, the two large chantries at the east end and the pulpit. This lack of interest is due to two factors, immediate post-reformation iconoclasm and the 'great scrape' of 1840. It is said that the whole church inside was then covered with whitewash, the removal of which was a major operation. The painted designs on the high vault were renewed at this time,[48] but it is thought that they are based on traces of thirteenth century work remaining. There is compensation for the bareness of the nave in the beautifully clear appearance of the plain walls of Doulting stone which have so remained during the century since they were cleaned. The Rood also has helped to relieve the monotony, and to remind the great crowds which come to see the clock that this is a Christian church. The removal of some tablets, however, particularly that to the Linleys and Mrs Sheridan from near the north door, is inexcusable.

CHANTRY ALTARS

There is confusion about the dedication of altars across the nave by the two chantries. Church, with much reason, considers that a pulpitum marking the end of the twelfth century choir, and with the great rood over, here stretched across the church, there being doors in the centre and in the two aisles. A charter of 1306 says that there were two altars *ad ingressum chori* in honour of our Lady and of St Andrew. Church[49] puts these on each side of a door in the centre of the nave, in addition to the two on the sites of the present chantry altars. The existence of the four altars he shows seems rather doubtful, i.e. from north to south (1) St Saviour, (2) our Lady, (3) St Andrew, (4) St Edmund of Canterbury. There is no evidence of the dedication to St Saviour. Many references to the Chantry of St Saviour show it to be in the 'chapel of Holy Cross in the north part of the church,' i.e. at the foot of the Chapter House stairs. It may be that the

altar in the Bubwith chantry was so dedicated after the
bishop was buried, and it is significant that the chapel of
his almshouse in Wells is dedicated to St Saviour, St Mary
and All Saints.[50] There seems no doubt that the altar in
the Sugar chantry was dedicated from the thirteenth century
to St Edmund, Archbishop, but we cannot be certain that
separate altars existed here for Our Lady and St Andrew.
They may have been used while the east end of the cathedral was closed for extension. The matter is further complicated by the fact that an important image of Our Lady
at which alms were offered for two centuries, and before
which Canon John de Hywysch (Hewish) wished to be buried
in 1361, was situated before the door of the choir.

Both chantries have the plan of an elongated octagon, the
two long sides, north and south, being divided into three
bays. Two of the resulting twelve bays, however, are filled
with the square sides of the nave piers, stripped or partially
stripped of their attached shafts. At each east end, the reredos
stretches across three divisions so that the interior plan is
almost rectangular.

The two chantries provide interesting examples of early and
late perpendicular work. Each bay may be regarded either
as a large two light window reaching down to the floor with
a heavy transom, or as a window standing on the transom
as a sill, with panelling underneath. Two-thirds of the lights
below the transom are filled with blank masonry but the
heads are rather archaic even for the time of Bubwith, and
they have been copied for the other chantry seventy years
later. The head is trefoiled but the openings are one centred
or circular and cusped, 3, 5, 3. In the Bubwith chantry the
same arrangement is repeated for the two main lights above,
except that the arches now spring from capitals almost as
in an Early English arcade. The tracery, however, is typically
early perpendicular of c. 1430, consisting of two trefoiled
lights. These are under a two centred arch, and above again
the tympanum is pierced with quatrefoils. There is then a
cornice of vine leaves, some moulding, and a final cresting
of closely packed finials. In both chantries only a section over
the altars is vaulted, and the cresting is carried across the

edge of the roof. The Bubwith vault is fairly plain, of a barrel type of eight curved panels with a quatrefoil design cut on them.

The reredos in the Bubwith chantry consisted of seven niches with canopies, the three central being under one canopy. It has been much cut back and damaged. There is a piscina on an attached shaft, damaged, and with a number of drain holes. Both chantries have iron stays running across the openings, but this was for structural purposes and not to prevent ingress. On June 22nd, 1489, Canon William Bocat, one of the executors of Treasurer Sugar prayed for leave to take down and remove the wooden chapel (presumably housing the altar of St Edmund) and to rebuild the same. The Dean and Chapter gave the permission.[51] Although it was much richer, care was taken to make the new chantry match the older one on the north and it is built on the same plan. In each bay, work below the transom is almost identical, with the curious circular head. This, however, has not been repeated for the main head of the Sugar window, which is of an orthodox late perpendicular pattern. The central mullion divides at tracery level, and continues in a Y form to meet the arch. Each of the two lights thus made are cinquefoiled and the ogee point continues upwards to divide the tracery into two rectangular openings, trefoil headed, but with no cusping at the base. Two similar openings are provided between the arms of the Y. The tympanum is finished with pierced quatrefoils, exactly as in the Bubwith chantry. The cornice consists firstly of a row of paterae in a deep hollow, then much plain moulding, surmounted by a course of pierced quatrefoils, finally topped with a cresting of rich finials linked at their points. On the outside of this chantry an additional very narrow panel is introduced between the main panels. This has a trefoil and finial at transom and tracery level. In front of the paterae and moulding of the cornice are a row of demi-angels with large wings holding shields. They have fillet and cross. Counting from the pulpit opening on the aisle side, the shields display (1) the arms of Sugar : *three sugar loafs, and in chief a doctor's cap;* (2) the Annunciation : a pot of lilies, with a detached wing on each side ; (3) the

arms of Glastonbury Abbey (one of the few remaining intact
in the county): *a cross flory, in dexter chief a demi-virgin
with child ppr.;* (4) a doctor's cap, and below very elaborate
initials HS.; (5) the Five Wounds of our Lord: hands and
feet with heart, pierced; (6) arms of the Deanery: *a saltire
betw. on the dexter two keys addorsed the bows interlaced,
and on the sinister a sword erect.* On the inner side of the
chantry we find: (1) the Deanery; (2) the Five Wounds;
(3) HS., (4) Sugar arms; (5) the Annunciation; (6) a Saltire.
This is ribbed and presumably is intended for the College of
Vicars. It is curiously now used by the bishop of the diocese.
Inside this chantry we find over the altar five equal niches,
the rich canopies of which are intact. They may have held
statues. Below them a stone shield has some now indecipherable carving upon it. Above are small angels holding shields
displaying the sugar arms and the initials HS. There is a
fine but orthodox fan vault over the altar in contrast with
the plain affair in the other chantry, and small piscina with
credence shelf.

THE GREAT NAVE PULPIT

Stairs have now been placed in the north-west bay of the
chantry leading up into the pulpit. This is very plain, but
effective, obviously of Renaissance date with panels and
deeply moulded cornice. On the front are carved the mutilated
arms of Bishop Knight, 1547: *per fess, a double headed eagle,
having on its breast a demi-rose and a demi-sun conjoined
in one.* The arms may be seen with their blazoning more
clearly in the window of the north choir aisle near the
modern pulpit.[52] They were given to the bishop by the
Emperor Maximilian in 1514 when he was acting as Apostolic
Protonotory and Ambassador of Henry VIII to the Emperor.
The pulpit is supposed to have been built during the life-
time of Knight which Godwin says 'hee caused to be built
for his tombe.' It is not known whether the bishop is in fact
buried here. Around the frieze of the entablature is the text
cut in the stone and coloured red: *'Preache thou the worde,
Be fervent in season and out of season. Reprove, rebuke, exhort,
with all longe sufferyng and doctryne. 2 Timo.'*

Among the sad remains of memorials in the floor of the nave, two are outstanding. Bubwith's chantry has been built partly upon three blocks of Purbeck Marble forming a life-size indent of a figure of Bishop Haselshaw, archdeacon, dean, and bishop, †1308. The whole memorial measures 181 by 76 inches and is surrounded by an inscription in Lombardic capitals. Each brass letter was set in a separate indent, a practice which was only in use for a short time, as it was found unsatisfactory, the letters being easily kicked out. It was thought that some might have been protected here by the later chantry, and investigation took place in 1925, when one only was found, the letter E and a double stop : . This has been left exposed by cutting away a stone of the chantry. The step also was taken up at this time to reveal the clear indent 'quondam.' The whole inscription can now be restored with tolerable certainty as *Walterus de Heselshaw quondam Bathoniensis et Wellensis Episcopus cuius anime propicietur deus Amen.* A very similar indent of a brass, but nearly a century later and smaller is found by the Sugar chantry and partly covered by the pulpit. This is to Bishop Ralph Erghum (†1400). It is much flaked and the inscription, which here would have been cut in brass strips without separate indents, has altogether vanished. There are a number of references however which fix this as the burial place of the bishop. Godwin says of him, *Sepultus jacet extra Capellam magno pulpito contiguam ad Septentrionem.* The bishop had the brass made in his life-time.[53]

The magnificent brass lectern was one of several gifts of Dean, afterwards Bishop Creyghton, at the Restoration of 1660. It is of the double medieval type and has to be approached by stairs. It was intended for the choir where it stood for a few years until it went out of use and was put in the Retro-choir until removed to the nave in this century. The inscription reads 'Dr Rob[t] Creyghton upon his return from fifteen years Exile, wth o[r] Soveraigne Lord Kinge Charles y[e] 2[d] made Deane of Wells, in y[e] yeare 1660, gave this Brazen Deske, wth God's holy worde thereon in the saide Cathedral Church.' *Gulielmus Borroughes Londini me fecit Ano dni 1661.*

CHAPTER IV

THE CHOIR IN THE FOURTEENTH
CENTURY

IT is perhaps idle to speculate over the date of the Lady
Chapel which was certainly finished by 1326, if not before.
The difficulty is no less in considering the extension of the
choir and the attendant chapels. If we try to picture the
appearance of the Early English east end before it was taken
down, we must consider two examples which remain to us,
Durham and Abbey Dore.[54] The former provides, in its great
chapel of the Nine Altars, an example which, though it was
nearly a century later than Wells, carried on the tradition
of a one-bay ambulatory. At Abbey Dore we are very close
in time to Wells, but here the east end, much smaller, consists of two bays, although under a single lean-to roof. One
of these is an ambulatory proper, and the other provides
altar recesses. There was a similar arrangement at Glastonbury, although this was adopted in the much later addition
of Abbot Monington. The question arises as to whether the
Wells ambulatory contained any chapels or altars. We have
no documentary references except to a Lady Chapel (II)
'behind the High Altar.'[55] This was later than the ancient
chapel, *juxta claustrum* (I), and earlier than the present chapel
(III). Clearly it was destroyed during the extension of the
choir.

Since the ambulatory was only one bay wide, it has been
assumed that this Lady Chapel was a more or less detached
building but approached from it. Church, following Willis,
gives a complete but quite conjectural plan.[56] Excavations
carried out in 1914 by Dean Robinson provided no support
for this theory. They showed the sleeper wall foundation of
the eastern arcade, and of the ambulatory east wall but not
the number of arches in the arcade. If there were three they
must have been very narrow, so there were probably two, involving a central pier behind the High Altar. Bilson points
out that there would have been serious roofing and vaulting

difficulties for a 'detached' Lady Chapel. Perhaps therefore
it was contrived within the ambulatory.

EASTWARD EXTENSION

We cannot really say when the great fourteenth century
eastward extension began at Wells, or which part was first
undertaken. This date would not have been much before 1320.
We also cannot know whether the old east end of the choir
was removed early in the proceedings, or left until the extension was complete. At some time the vaults of the old choir
were removed, and the three extra bays, with a triple arcade
at the east end, all in a fully developed Decorated style, were
raised. There is no triforium in the new section of the Choir.
The capitals have shrunk to mere tokens, and in fact moulding runs directly from the bases to the windows, thus dividing
the new space into three cells. The vault springs from corbels
supported by triple shafts of Purbeck marble. These rise from
the pier bases, with two annulations, the first at capital level.
The characteristic feature of the extension is the deep tabernacle work which Pevsner calls a grille, between the arcade
(no tympanum) and the clerestory. This consists of provision
for statues on pillar bases, standing under canopies. No figures
were ever executed except those over the High Altar, which
were placed here in the present century and much improve
the appearance of the choir.[57] The tracery of the great east
window has been described as semi-Perpendicular. This may
be, but it does in fact resemble that of simpler windows of
the Lady Chapel. The seven (instead of five) main lights are
cinquefoiled, the centre ones being carried much higher than
the outer pairs. The outer mullions of these centre lights
reach up to the main arch of the window, a Perpendicular
arrangement. Otherwise the openings of the tracery form
simple cusped figures with a mid-fourteenth century feeling.
There is reason to think that the glass is contemporary with
the window, and Dean Woodforde dates it at *c*. 1339.

The windows of the clerestory contain characteristic Decorated tracery, except that in the six inserted in the old walls
it is primitive and plain. Outside, the old drip stone is retained and the newer windows fit very badly under it. There

is a pronounced walk running round in front of the clerestory
and this enters each deep splay of the window under an ogee
arch and finial, with a similar but blank arch in the space
above.

The new high vault of the choir, although unmistakably
lierne, is unique. There are no ridge ribs either at the centre
or for the windows. The transverse ribs are broken by large
quadrilaterals and these are heavily cusped inside. The bosses
are large, without figures, and have been regilded. There are
no intermediate ribs, so that only three spring from each
corbel and the transverse ones fail to give any impression of
division into cells. In consequence much of the roof is left
flat and bare, apparently without support giving a tunnel
like effect.

The treatment of the three older western bays in order to
make them fit in with the new work is ingenious. The main
walls were left intact outside right up to the corbel table.
Inside, below clerestory level, the old triforium has been
filled in. Traces of this filling may be seen on blank wall
spaces next the crossing, and it is plain enough from the
back in the roof space. Shallow tabernacle work has been
inserted to match as far as possible the grille for statues which
fills the space between arcade and clerestory in the new part.
The arches are blank and there is insufficient depth for
statues. The vaulting shafts have here to spring from the foot
of this tabernacle work, since the outer triplet of the old
piers below is occupied supporting the third order of the
main arcade. The work consists in each bay of three principal
panels with ogee arch and finial, flanked by two smaller
ones. There is also a cornice pierced with quatrefoil openings
and embattled. On some of the machicolations are found
crosses similar to those on the bishop's throne below. They
were also on the original cresting, now destroyed, of the wall
behind the high altar. This detail serves to indicate a similar
date for all three features. Rather curiously, the whole of
the sham ornament rises considerably higher than the new
work it is intended to imitate. Probably it was not thought
worth while to lower the level of the old clerestory passage
to which it reaches.

The work of the third bay is different and more elaborate than that of the two westernmost bays. The cornice is carried forward, and the finials are made so large that the supporting ogees must needs bend forward to contain them. The finials in the genuine canopy work farther east become small again. This more elaborate third bay corresponds with the position of the original High Altar, and it is just possible that it was made so for this reason, just as a roof often changes over the rood loft. Such an explanation invites the assumption that the old part of the choir was changed first, and then remained in use before the dividing wall was removed.

In the 'ambulatory' bay in the south choir aisle, between the bench and the window sill, are definite signs, both inside and out, of an arched opening. This may be a blocked-up Low Side Window, or an opening left to remove debris when the old east wall was pulled down.

The whole choir suffered greatly from a drastic 'restoration' in 1848, and the only remaining piece of furniture is the throne, of conventional fourteenth century workmanship. Its front, however (with the curious stone door) probably dates from the Restoration (1661). Opposite, and protruding into the choir, is the pulpit memorial to Dean Jenkins, † 1851.

It will be remembered that the old ritual choir extended westwards over the crossing as far as the end of the first bay of the nave.[58] In 1326 we learn that the stalls therein were *ruinosi et deformes* and that the dignitaries were ordered to construct their own new ones in the choir, now east of the pulpitum. Each person was to spend thirty shillings *in stallo suo faciendo*. Presumably the stalls were of wood and survived until 1848. A plan of them is given by Reynolds. This allows for the accommodation of such picturesque figures as the abbots of Bec, Muchelney and Athelney.

These stalls were arranged in front of the main choir piers in the usual manner. A section of them is illustrated by Britton,[59] and there appears to have been a single row of sub stalls in front. The original stalls of 1325 very probably had the high canopies we now see in other cathedrals, but a large gallery was constructed in place of them. Those seated therein looked down upon the choir below through screen work of Perpendicular design. This arrangement was unique for a church of the collegiate nature of Wells. Quite a lot of the screen survives and panels have been used for various purposes in and out of the cathedral. Some now adjoin St John Baptist Chapel and others form an entrance screen to the north transept. Further panels may be found in such places as the organ seat of Shepton Mallet church. The loss of this unique feature of the choir is deplorable, and characterizes the destructive nature of the restoration of 1848.[60] The misericords to both ranges, stalls and sub stalls, are preserved in the present arrangement.

The new stone stalls are set back between the piers, and this has involved a reduction in numbers so that the names of two prebendaries appear on many of them. All this work seems to have been done to provide extra room for a congregation displaced from the galleries. The Mayor and Corporation of Wells had specially constructed seats between the High Altar and the north choir aisle. These too were probably destroyed in 1848 and the whole presbytery was literally scraped clean at this time. The tombs of Bishops Still and Kidder were removed from south and north of the altar and placed in the chapels of the north transept.

BISHOP BECKINGTON—BENEFACTOR

At the same time the magnificent canopy to the tomb of Bishop Beckington was taken away to form a covering for a Gurney stove in St Calixtus' Chapel, and the effigy pushed out into the aisle. The canopy was happily rescued and restored by Dean Robinson in 1927. At this time the vault was entered. The episcopal ring remained and is now preserved in the library.[61]

The cadaver type of tomb was not uncommon at this time and was adopted by a later Bishop of Bath and Wells, Fox (†1528), after he had been translated to Winchester. Beckington, although a native of a village of that name near Frome and of fairly humble origin, was Secretary to Henry VI and Ambassador to France. He was typical of the statesman-bishop of those days, but he did not forget Wells, building part of the cloisters and the gateways, and improving the college of Vicars Choral.

The effigy of alabaster rests on a table tomb of Dundry freestone. On each of the six pillars supporting the slab is a feathered demi-angel with open wings and fillet and cross on forehead. The figure is beautifully coloured and in good condition. It is fully vested in amice, fringed maniple and stole, mitra pretiosa crocketed, with fringed infulae, tunicle, dalmatic and chasuble. The broken staff has the sudery. The high iron railings round the tomb or chantry are exceptionally fine. They were coloured but have been blacked over. Their restoration was not complete in 1927 and portions are in use as gates to the chapels in the south transept. This tomb was erected in 1451 and consecrated in 1452 by the bishop himself, who did not die until 1465. The great canopy to the altar seems very advanced in design for its date, and may be the result of the bishop's cosmopolitan activities. The main arch is four-centred and has on it two angels identical with those of the tomb. The north and south sides are really Perpendicular windows. They have very low transoms with what is sometimes called 'west Somerset' tracery of quatre-foils below the transoms. They have been modified on the north side so that a celebrant might have a clear view of the High Altar, so avoiding simultaneous consecration. The vault appears to have the pendants usually associated with the next century.

HIGH ALTAR AND SANCTUARY

We know next to nothing as to the nature of the High Altar reredos.[73] It may have been quite simple, judging from pieces of iron which indicate an attachment between the two central piers. The plain wall behind had, until the eighteenth century, a door in the centre hidden by the altar. This was removed, and Claver Morris's large monumental tablet erected in its place, to be later taken with all the others to the cloisters. The wall is built for the most part of cross hatched stones and some of these are found in the screen immediately to the south. It appears likely that it was made of debris from the older Early English east end of the choir. Both ends were renewed in 1848, but there does not appear to have been any change in its position. The fourteenth century wall had a plain castellated cresting, but this was changed during the restoration and made much more elaborate, like that under the great east window above. It has recently been removed altogether.

Attached to the screen in the south aisle is a rubbing of a brass stolen from the cathedral in the last century and supposed to have been in this position. It is now in the British Museum and commemorates Canon and Treasurer John Bernard (†1459).

In the centre of the choir between the choristers' seats, a new stone has been cut over the reputed burial place of Bishop Jocelin de Wells, builder of the West Front and the Palace. There is no record of excavation and the stone is now covered by carpet.

The fine pair of candlesticks on the High Altar are silver gilt. There is a similar pair in Bristol Cathedral, otherwise the arrangement of three legs is rare. They were the gift of Mrs. Agnes Tucker of Colyton, Devon, in 1789 and were gilded by the gift of Mary Lean in 1883. They bear the maker's mark of Gabriel Sleath and the Hall Mark for 1712. The Cross which is copper gilt was given as a memorial to Bishop Harry Thomas in 1955.

In the north choir aisle we find the large alabaster effigy of Bishop Ralph of Shrewsbury, †1363. It has been treated with scant respect, having lost its 'grates' or railings and been removed hither from its position immediately in front of the High Altar in 1550. It is likely that this bishop was responsible for the completion of the choir, which would account for his burial in such a position. The effigy is fully vested in apparelled alb, amice, maniple and stole, the last two with expanded ends and fringe, and chasuble, tunicle, dalmatic, jewelled gloves, mitra preciosa, and staff (broken) with sudery.

Another very similar tomb but a little later is that of Bishop Harewell (†1386). This is to be found between St Calixtus' Chapel and the south choir aisle. Except for details of ornament, the figure is vested exactly as is that of Bishop Ralph. The feet are resting on two hares, a reference to the bishop's name. This monument seems at one time to have been elsewhere in the south aisle, but has since been restored to its rightful position. The figure is bulky, and there may be an intention to portray a fat man; but the result is not too happy and there is a monstrous appearance about the head.

Both these effigies are of alabaster from the Midlands—probably from Chellaston in Derbyshire. The problem of the transport of such large blocks of stone arises. We know that the port of Reckley on the Axe near Axbridge, now disappeared, was used to import roofing stone for the Manor of Wells, and it is quite likely that the effigies came that way. The route obviated haulage over the steep roads of the Mendips. The stone would leave Chellaston by way of the Trent to the Humber, or overland direct to the Severn. It should again be noted that modern names dating from the nineteenth century have been cut on these and many other tombs.[62]

EASTERN CHAPELS—ST JOHN BAPTIST

The chapel at the end of the south choir aisle is dedicated to St John Baptist. The tracery of the windows is in a well defined mid-Decorated style conforming to the general date for the east end of *c*. 1330. Ogee curves are present, in contrast to the windows of the Lady Chapel adjoining. Between these chapels there stands a somewhat curious monument which acts as a screen. On the back is a design incorporating the Agnus Dei, and probably referring to the dedication of the chapel. This is said to have been restored by Dean Goodenough.

The tomb chest, surmounted by a plain slab of Purbeck Marble, is of an early Perpendicular date. The very high and elaborate pinnacles appear at first sight to be rather early in style but there is a strong resemblance to the infilling of the central tower windows *c*. 1360. There is no justification, however, for the ascription of the tomb to Bishop Bytton I (†1264). According to Leland and others, this bishop was buried, presumably after a translation, in the centre of the Lady Chapel III: *jacet cum imagine aerea in Capella B. Mariae ad orientalem partem ecclesiae de Wells,* and there is a somewhat inconclusive account of the excavation of his grave in 1727.[63] Later writers have supposed that the monument was moved to one side to clear the Lady Chapel, but there seems no doubt that it was then completely destroyed.

We are in the same difficulty as before in assigning the tomb to any likely person, since the tombs of all the bishops can be accounted for. Jewers suggests Canon John Marcel, †1341, who founded a chantry in the neighbouring chapel of St Katherine. On the bench of the chapel for many years lay the effigies of two of the Saxon bishops, later restored to their proper positions by Dean Robinson. The east end was occupied by the large monument by Chantrey to Mr Phelips of Montacute, now in the cloisters.

The present altar furnishings have recently been provided by the C.E.M.S. of the diocese, and the former reredos, contrived by Dean Robinson, has been removed to the adjoining chapel of St Katherine. This is made up of panels from the galleries of the choir with the inscription *Agnus Dei, qui tollis peccata mundi* added. It thus appertains to St John Baptist, and may well in the future cause confusion about the dedications of these chapels.

EASTERN CHAPELS—ST KATHERINE

The transept chapel now containing the St John reredos is dedicated to St Katherine or, more precisely, as we learn from Dean Gunthorpe's will, in the names *sanctissimarum virginum, Katerine, Margarete, beatissime Marie Magdalene et Marie Egipcian et omnium sanctorum et sanctarum Dei.*[64] It is separated from that of St John Baptist by the fine tomb of Bishop Drokensford (†1329). This is one of a pair, the other being exactly symmetrically placed in the north choir transept, and will be discussed later. In both cases the bases are of Blue Lias surmounted by a nondescript arcading in Doulting stone below a thin slab of Purbeck Marble on which the effigy rests. Both had canopies which were lost in the eighteenth century.

The figure of Drokensford is in excellent condition and the original colouring remains, recently restored under the direction of Professor Tristram. The bishop is vested in apparelled amice and alb, maniple, dalmatic, chasuble, no tunicle, mitre

E

without infulae, and staff (broken). He was keeper of the wardrobe under Edward I. The effigy was probably made in Bristol of Dundry stone. The panels round the tomb chest have ogee heads with finials. They are flanked by buttresses, and the spandrels are adorned with heater shaped shields, blazoned with two coats of arms placed alternately : (1) *Quarterly 1 and 4 argent, 2 and 3 gules, four swan's heads couped addorsed and counterchanged.* (2) *Ermine, on a shield gu., two buck's heads caboshed or. (Popham).* This tomb was formerly attributed to Bishop Bytton I, adding to the general confusion, but Jewers discovered that the first shield, although not in Papworth, is undoubtedly that of Drokensford, since it appears in perfect condition on a seal attached to a deed of gift from one Philip de Drokensford, first cousin of the bishop, to John de Godelee, Dean of Wells. This also illustrates the close association of Drokensford with Godelee, bishop and dean, now lying under this pair of tombs in the two transepts of the choir they did so much to build.

Along the southern wall of this chapel lies the tomb of a greater statesman and Renaissance scholar, Dean Gunthorpe, †1498. He held many offices in Rome, was Lord High Almoner to Edward IV and Warden of King's Hall, Cambridge. The last ten years of his life he spent quietly in Wells, although he did a considerable amount of building at the deanery.[65] This is a severely plain and heavily moulded table tomb, the only decoration being five 8-cusped openings on the front. In these are shields with the following in the first four : (1) The Deanery of Wells. (2) *Gunthorpe: Quarterly 1 and 4, Within a bordure engrailed sable, a chevron between three guns:* (2 and 3) *A chevron between three leopards' heads.* (3) *gules, a chevron ermine between three crosses botonny or.* (4) *Gules, on a bend compony argent and azure between two lions' heads erased of the second three leopards' faces, a bordure like the bend.* These arms were borne by Thomas Gunthorpe, *Prioris de Novo Loco in Schirewood,* i.e. Newstead Abbey, near Nottingham, in 1467. In the fifth panel are the letters I.G. in the form of a monogram. Traces of original colouring remained and these have recently been restored : the tinctures given are those apparent before restora-

tion. Dean Woodforde considers that there are evidences of
something having been attached to the wall above the tomb,
and that this may have been a representation of the Nativity
mentioned in the dean's will, in which he directs that he
should be buried *in capella sancte Katerine in parte australi
summi altaris subtus imaginem beate Marie le Gesnian*. A
very curious piece of medieval ironwork is attached to the
tomb. It may well be part of a pricket to hold candles burning before this image.[66]

On the west wall of St Katherine's chapel are two interesting brasses mercifully brought here during the great destruction of monuments in 1848. The earlier of these is to Henry
Hawley. A shield bears : *(Vert) a saltire engrailed (arg), a
crescent for difference.* The inscription reads : *Henry Hawley
Armiger qui obüt octavo die Februarij XII Anno dñi 1573.*[67]
This brass was formerly against a pillar in the north transept,
then on the wall in the same place, and lastly on the south
wall of the Lady Chapel. Another brass, that to Humphrey
Willis, and of greater interest, is nearby. It shows a young
man kneeling in a field. Behind him are the toys of this
world, a grand hat and shoes, a broken sword, cards, dice,
racquet and ball, and a fiddle. In front we see a set of gleam-
ing armour labelled *Armatura Dei: Hanc mihi.* The Hebrew
name JHWH (Jehovah) is engraved on a segment of the
sun in the left top corner, and two angels are shown emerging
from the clouds. One is offering a laurel wreath, labelled
Vicisti recipe, and the other a book with the words *Petenti
dabitur.* Between them is an open book and in capital letters
on its leaves *Verbum Vitae.* The man appears to be saying
Da mihi Domine, and behind him is a broken tree indicating
his early death at the age of twenty-eight. It is labelled *Fracta*
and the remaining trunk *Non Mortua.* In the roots are the
words *spe vivo.* From a branch of the tree hangs a shield
and on it the arms of Carrick : *(or) a fess dancetté between
three talbots passant(sa) on an escutcheon of pretence.*
Humphrey Willis is shown clean shaven with hair covering his
ears. He wears a ruff, tunic, breeches, stockings, elaborate
garters and shoes. Below is this straightforward inscription :
Hic situs est Humfredus Willis armiger filius Hum: Willis ar.

qui obiit Octob: 21 Anno Aetatis suae 28: An. Dñi 1618. Hoc piae memoriae sacrum, lugens uxor posuit. There then follows a somewhat obscure Latin verse:

> *Deterior pars viva mei, meliorq sepulta est*
> *Ut peream vivo, vivat ut ille perit*
> *Terra tibi hos cineres comēndo meosq dolores*
> *Huic cineri donec tradar et ipsa cinis.*

Finally in small italics: *Optabit melius T.P. consanguineus.*[68]

Another monument in the south choir aisle deserving careful attention is that to Bishop Bytton II, †1274. Of this bishop's burial place Godwin says: *Monumentum ejus situm est inter duas columnas ab australi parte chori ubi marmor videmus pontificis imaginem habens insculptam.* Thus until 1848, the slab lay between the first and second piers from the crossing exactly in line with that of Bishop Jocelin in the centre of the choir, before the old High Altar. It was disturbed at this time and in the stone coffin was found a skeleton in perfect order, an iron ring, a small wooden pastoral staff, and a leaden tablet inscribed in Lombardic characters *Hic jacet Willelmus de Button secundus Bathoniensis et Wellensis episcopus sepultus XII die Decembris anno domini MCCLXXIIII.* The grave items were apparently reburied. It was noted that the teeth were perfect and this was associated with Godwin's story that 'many superstitious people especially such as were troubled with the toothache, were wont (even of late years) to frequent much the place of his burial.'

The large single stone of Blue Lias was thus moved a few feet away out into the aisle. It is said to be the earliest incised tomb in England. The bearded figure of the bishop, pontifically vested (without tunicle) in the act of benediction, is beautifully cut. Curiously there are no feet. The Reverend John Bowen, writing about 1800, describes the removal in 1748 (Church) of the High Altar reredos and the canopies of the tombs of Bishops Drokensford and Bytton II. This slab may have had a canopy, but it seems more likely that the writer was referring to some other tomb.

EASTERN CHAPELS—ST STEPHEN AND CORPUS CHRISTI

The north choir aisle ends with the chapel of SS Stephen (Pope) and John Evangelist, often ascribed only to St Stephen. It has recently been refurnished by the Mothers' Union of the diocese and has a fine parclose screen by Sir Ninian Comper showing the adoration of the Magi.[69]

Two features common to these eastern chapels may be noted. The bench has been carried right round the eastern wall, so that the original altar, detached and perhaps of wood, must have stood at some distance from the wall. The piscina in the eastern wall had its large ogee arch or label cut off at the reformation, and the hole filled up. This and the bowl is a restoration, but the inner arch is original.

The next chapel in the north choir transept is dedicated in honour of Corpus Christi, and now appropriately used for the reservation of the Blessed Sacrament. If we reconsider for a moment the chapels in the *main* north transept of the church we find that the first (south) has the dedication Corpus Christi *subtus campanile,* the second being Holy Cross. Yet we find that Bishop Cornish, † 1513, calls them St David and Holy Cross. The inference is clearly that when the new east end was built the Corpus Christi altar was moved to one of the new chapels, the old chapel becoming St David. We find confirmation of this in 1331, when the obit of Dean Godelee is being arranged in a new Corpus Christi chapel *ad altare in honorem corpus et Sanguinis Christi constructum, et adhuc dedicandum.* This entry in the great white book of the cathedral, *Liber Albus I* (R1 ff.179d–80), is of particular importance as it not only fixes the dedication of this chapel but gives us the only firm date for any of the building of the fourteenth century east end. So this choir transept was built but not dedicated by 1331. Two years later Godelee was buried in it, across the entrance, in a tomb matching that of his bishop, Drokensford, across the church. The figure, however, is unpainted and there is no blazoning of arms; but otherwise the details are the same.

The canopies over the two tombs were probably removed in 1800, although there is a ledger stone of earlier date over the canopy foundations on the north side. The figure is that

of a priest fully vested and of mid-fourteenth century date.
There is a legend painted on the bevel of the Purbeck Marble
slab, and Dean Robinson in 1925 thought he could read :
HIC: JACET: MAGISTER: JOH . . . It can only be reported forty years later that four letters remain : *IC: JA*.
There can be little doubt, however, but that this is the tomb
of Godelee.

A most interesting story about this chapel and, incidentally
further confirmation as to its dedication, is to be found in
two poems written by a native of Wells, Prebendary Alexan-
der Huish (1595–1668). In the first he says :

> *Corporis hanc Christi titulo notam esse Capellam*
> *Inscriptum fragili legimus ante vitro.*

Unfortunately no trace of ancient glass now remains in the
chapel.

The second poem refers to the arched recess in the north
wall in which Huish found a fresco : *infra partem muri
arcutum extra Chorum, Capellam Corporis Christi.* This was
of a crucifix, surrounded by the instruments of the passion.
As soon as the then dean heard about it, he had it destroyed.
Below, Huish says there was a sepulchre (*sepulcrum*).

This cannot refer to the existing effigy since it is shown by
Carter to be in the north-west corner. Moreover, it does not
fit the recess and is a century out of date with the canopy,
which is rather plain Perpendicular work. Whether Huish
means that the sepulchre was part of the painting we cannot
know. If it were an actual representation of Christ's tomb,
a good case can be made out for the whole recess being an
Easter Sepulchre. It is in the right position, but we have to
remember that a like claim may be made for the tomb of
Bishop Cornish in the north transept.

The effigy of a priest now in the recess is almost certainly
that of John de Middleton, who was made Chancellor of
Wells in 1337.[70]

On the floor of Corpus Christi Chapel, under the carpet
in front of the altar, we have the only medieval brass remaining in the cathedral, but this unfortunately lacks an inscription. It is a half-effigy, *c.* 1460, of a priest in a cope, com-

plete with morse and mascule. Under the cope we see the fur lining of the almuce with its two stole-like ends. At the wrists are the sleeves of a surplice and cassock and possibly of a sub-tunic. This probably represents a canon, and is a valuable record of fifteenth century choir dress.

The carving of the Ascension over the altar was moved here recently from the cloisters where the indent may be seen near the vault by the door leading to Stillington's chapel. There it would hardly have been *in situ* but may have been put out to preserve it from iconoclasts. Our Lord is shown ascending through the clouds in the usual manner. Eleven apostles are seen, all in beards, and all uniform except that some carry their symbols. In front are two female figures beautifully draped, probably our Lady and St Mary Magdalene. A palm branch lies on the ground between them and there are vestiges of colouring.

Two episcopal monuments remain in the chapel. One of these, a rather clumsy chest tomb, is to Bishop Berkeley, †1581. This was brought here some time after the end of the eighteenth century, when Carter's plan was made, from a position north of the High Altar. A difficulty arises about the former position of the monument, since that of Kidder is shown by Britton (1823) in this position facing south. Perhaps it was behind in the aisle, having displaced one of the Saxon bishops. Berkeley came of a Norfolk family said to have been connected with that of Gloucestershire. The descent is certainly claimed on the tomb where the Berkeley arms are repeated with a rose on the chevron for difference. Cassan, however, denies the connection and says that the bishop's name did not appear at the Herald's College. On the top of this table tomb, round the margin, runs a curious inscription, intended to give the year of death by means of numeral letters, coloured red, but it is no longer possible to follow this devise.

Spiritus erupto salvus Gilberte Novembre
Carcere principio en aethere Barkle crepat
Añ: dāt ista salutis

'These give the year of Salvation,' mccccllllvvvvviiiiii, 1581.

The words *principio en* have been altered to *tristis in hoc* without altering the numeration. On the middle of this slab is the verse :

> *Vixi videtis praemium*
> [83] *Luxi redux qui fascibus*
> *Pro captu agendo praesulis*
> *Septem per annos triplices.*

The words *Vixi, Luxi* give 83, the bishop's age, although Cassan says he was 80. The last line records that he reigned as bishop for twenty-one years.

The other bishop's tomb in this chapel is to the Restoration Dean and Bishop, Creyghton († 1672). It is a beautiful work in marble and again looks as if it did not properly belong in its north-eastern corner. We do not know, however, that it ever stood anywhere else. Although the effigy is not dressed in the eucharistic vestments it is remarkably carefully treated, and shows an exact knowledge of the traditional garments of the church, if not by the bishop then by the statuary. It is vested in cassock, amice, alb and girdle, cope with jewelled morse, skull cap and mitra pretiosa having infulae. The mitre is low compared with those worn by continental bishops at this time, but the staff has rich Renaissance ornament, although without sudery. The bishop is shown as a big man, six feet three inches tall with a strong Scottish face, thin moustache and the tiny lip beard of the cavalier. He was a relation of the King, had been abroad with the court and appointed to the deanery on the murder of his predecessor, Raleigh. When he took possession in 1661 he had a heavy task of restoration, since the bishop, Piers, was aged and incapable. On the death of the latter in 1670 he very exceptionally succeeded as bishop, but only lived for a further two years. A long Latin inscription formed a pediment to the tomb but was removed in 1848, together with an adjoining monument to his wife. Both were restored in the south cloister walk by Dean Robinson.

A number of medieval tiles with armorial bearings are on the floor of the chapel. As there are none elsewhere in the cathedral, they have no doubt been collected here at some time. The families represented seem to have no very definite connection with Wells and the tiles may well have been manufactured for general use, at least in the West Country. Jewers gives a complete account with speculations about them. The Jacobean screen for this chapel was brought from a farm out-house at Baltonsborough. It had no previous connection with the cathedral.

CHAPTER V

THE CHAPTER HOUSE AND LADY CHAPEL

FOURTEENTH CENTURY

THE position of the Chapter House in monasteries had been firmly established in Norman times as adjoining the south transept of the church, and leading out of the east cloister walk. Its place in secular communities, however, was different. They did not often possess cloisters, and the room is usually found near the north transept, as originally at Wells. The shape of the earlier monastic Chapter Houses was rectangular, with perhaps an apse, while that of the secular houses was polygonal. The latter shape is generally considered to be an English innovation following the development of the Gothic style. The earliest example which remains, however, is at Worcester, built early in the twelfth century and this is circular inside but polygonal outside. As it was for the use of a Benedictine community, it is in the orthodox position adjoining the east cloister walk.

Probably the first secular House to be built in England was at Beverley. This was octagonal, but only the foundations remain. From the staircase, however, the shafts of which have the squared abaci and water-holding bases, we may take the date to be not later than 1230. Note that the foundations and lower walls were built at Wells at about the same time, although the House was completed much later. Wells thus provides the earliest remaining layout of a secular polygonal chapter house in England, although Lincoln came soon after.

We have seen that one of the most significant signs of the 'break' in the nave building at Wells was an abrupt change from cross to vertical hatching of the stone. We find that the whole of the lower part of the undercroft to the Chapter House, up to the window sills, is built of cross hatched stone. Moreover the base of the vaulting shafts built into the interior of this octagonal wall are water-holding, a sure indication of an early thirteenth century date. In fact this hatching goes six or seven courses higher in the one side of the octagon which forms the end of the passage. Cross hatching is also present in the passage and on the exterior western face of the staircase, but is not so clear as in the undercroft, nor is it possible to say exactly where it ends. It may be that the passage and the base of the staircase was built at an intermediate time when both types of face were being used.

It would seem however, that the Chapter House complex was not visualized by the planners of Reginald's church, since the door to its undercroft has been cut through his earlier wall. Also, the door to the Chapter House stairs is so insignificant because it may once have led to a small vestry, having been adapted for its present use. This is clear from a comparison with an identical arrangement in the south transept (St Martin's Chapel). The roof marks of this vestry still exist at the foot of the chapter house staircase, as does a blocked up window. Curiously however it was higher than the vestry on the south, although it is most unlikely that there was formerly a door into the church at this point as has been suggested. The strongest argument against accepting an early date for the undercroft lay-out is found in the design of the plinth and buttress footings. The latter, however, here perform rather a different function from those in the nave. We have also to remember that the plinth of the western part of the nave is, like much of the other work, probably deliberately archaic. A break would have looked awkward, whereas it would not matter so much in a virtually detached building like the undercroft. The two types of plinth may be examined where they join by the north transept under the clock. There is no sign of cross-hatching on the massive central or other columns of the undercroft. These works belong to a later date in the century, as does the doorway from the north choir aisle with its lias shafts.

The sequence of events would seem to be as follows. Not long before the break in the building of the nave it was decided that the church required a chapter house which was laid out and built so far as the window sills of the undercroft. Quite possibly the latter, if not the House itself, was intended to be a separate building. After the break, a new regime concentrated on finishing the nave and building the West Front.

Work was not resumed on the Chapter house complex until later in the century, about 1285. To this later period of building belong the central and subsidiary piers and the upper half of the walls.

THE UNDERCROFT

A feature of the undercroft is the magnificent pair of doors fixed in series at the entrance. The inner one of these has fine thirteenth century ironwork and elaborate safety devices. Thus the bolt holes in the masonry are lined with iron, and there is provision for a detachable central post as well as cross bars. All these devices clearly operate from the inside, and the doors must have been fastened by someone within. How then did he get out of the undercroft? No sign of any other doorway exists, although there was preserved here a small door made of iron plates, described in detail in the *Archaeological Journal* for 1890. This may have closed another way out, but the explanation of Dr Dearmer that a guard slept within seems the most likely.

The windows of the undercroft are heavily defended by double gratings of iron. Curiously, they vary in size in an irregular manner owing to different depths of sill. A similar defence is provided for the passage (now sacristy), so it would seem that this was also used as a treasury, although outside the double doors of the undercroft itself. The passage has many points of interest. It may have been built after the undercroft was finished, assuming this latter building to have been detached from the church. This would account for the elaborate double door defence against the inside of the cathedral. The vault here would indicate a date after 1250 as would the bases of the shafts and their circular abaci. Other features however, such as the floriated capitals and design of the bosses, and some cross hatching are hardly as late as 1280 previously suggested.

On the west side, the passage runs along the earlier transept wall, and the spaces between the buttresses have been utilized as aumbrys. Here there are normal freestone shafts to the corbels supporting the vault. On the east side, however, the corbels are supported by large heads. Every other one of these is upside down. It may be that a plain wall was desired on this side for some purpose not now apparent, perhaps for wooden cupboards. The beautiful little stone lantern at the far end of the passage should be noted, and some old tombstones have been used for the flooring near the door, one apparently of the fourteenth century. Their inscriptions cannot now be read.

We may consider the vault of the passage. Just inside the door is a small cell contrived in the thickness of the wall. It is supported on some odd corbels. One is a head with enormous cheeks, another is a head upside down, and a third consists of two dragons biting each other. Some of the bosses in the main vault are interesting. Number two from the entrance has on it a fine *Agnus Dei,* and the next the heads of two men joined at the crown. The fourth is a man seated, engaged on some occupation not now apparent, and the next an ox. The last is curious as it has male and female heads both on snakes' bodies.

The undercroft housed some interesting relics, as well as the early iron door already mentioned. There was a cannon ball of which no record remains. It may belong to the period of the 'siege of Wells,' during the Great Rebellion. We saw also a number of massive stone coffins, some of which were made for priests, since space is provided on one side for the mortuary chalice and paten. Our chief interest however centred in the remarkable wooden hanging pyx. This consists of an octagon of three tiers of pierced windows following exactly the design of late thirteenth century stonework. The centre tier contains plate tracery, and there are shafts with plain circular capitals. The whole is four feet in height and about one and a half feet wide. At the top is a crest of tre-foiled woodwork. The base is open and there are signs of ironwork which may have allowed an inner vessel to be drawn up and down. Other examples of such pyxes, although later in date, may be seen in Tewkesbury and at Milton Abbas, Dorset. These relics have been dispersed but may in future be available for the public to see.

The stairs to the Chapter House have no connection with the undercroft passage and were made after taking down the vestry which served the chapels of the north transept. Their interest lies in the magnificent sweep of steps contrived to turn a right angle, and continued at a much later date to the road bridge; and in the three unique windows. A most instructive comparison can be made between these staircase windows and those of the Chapter House itself from the area of the north porch where they are seen one above the other.

We have in the former a perfect example of very fully developed *plate* tracery and in the latter one of mature *geometrical* design, both of course of the Decorated period. We can see the same essential design, based on the circle, in both, yet there must be a quarter of a century difference in date. The workers of 1310 have, in the interval, mastered the principle of stone tracery, and we see signs between the circles of a freedom of design which in the next few years was to become Flamboyant in Europe and Reticulated in England. The windows of the staircase are plain outside and consist of two lancets subdivided so that four main lights result.

Over the two main lancets a circle has been cut containing three other cusped circles, and this is repeated over the two sub-lancets below. Single attached shafts with plain capitals and bases support the arches of the main lancets. Inside, these windows are sumptuously treated and appear to be later in design. The jambs to the window arch are splayed widely so as to expose a large surface, each consisting of six shafts. Three of these have capitals of the upright fern design characteristic of the stairs and chapter house, and plain bases. They support an arch of three orders over the window. They have shafts of blue lias, the method of using this stone for insetting having been continued from the west front. The remaining three shafts of the window jambs run up without base or capital. If we consider the structure of the window itself, we find that the mullions all carry shafts with base and capital. This practice was abandoned a few years later in the Chapter House. The centre mullion is wide and carries a triplet of shafts with capitals and bases supporting the main and subsidiary lancet arches. All four lancets are cinquefoiled inside but plain outside. This, and the definite moulding to the 'tracery,' gives a much richer appearance to the window from the interior. Dr Robinson considers that stained glass was first used in the cathedral at this point and that it was fixed into wooden frames and not directly to the masonry, as soon became the universal custom. If this was so, the frames must have fitted on the outside and the prevailing western wind would have kept them pressed against the inner cusping. No stained glass remains in the lower lights and only a few scraps in the tracery where the usual method of inserting the glass is adopted.

THE CHAPTER HOUSE

It is generally accepted that the Room itself, including the lobby, was not begun before the turn of the century. We find on reaching the vestibule a definite extension of the use of the Blue Lias. The central columns of both trumeaux consist of double monoliths of lias, placed back to back. The resulting awkward joint was opened out and filled with an ornamental cement of calcite. The jambs of both doorways have the same construction, and the capitals, for the first and last time wholly of lias, have a design of fern leaves and grapes. The panel-like arrangement on each side of the vestibule may be a slightly later addition. A shaft of Purbeck marble attached to the inner trumeau is almost certainly a (mistaken) restoration. There are benches on each side and signs of a wooden screen inside the outer archway. This may have been the mounting for a pair of doors, and it is said, on the authority of a former guide book, that they were removed and used for the canon's house next the Lady Chapel. Measurement shows this to have been possible.

The Chapter Room itself consists essentially of fifty-one stalls raised above a wide bench, seven in each of the eight sides, with the exception of the entrance bay, which has two. The centre seat, opposite the door, seems always to have been reserved for the bishop who, however, has doubtful jurisdiction in the chapter. In post-reformation times the stonework at the back of this seat was painted red, with a St Andrew's cross in the tympanum on one side. It seems likely that there was a bishop's arms on the other side, but no trace remains. Above, standing on the window ledge, is a Royal Achievement of Arms, painted on stone, of James I (or possibly James II). Below, and along the edge of the sill, we find an extra and unique motto : *Jacobus Rex ecclesiae nutritius*. Modern brass plates have been inserted for the dignitaries and prebendaries.

Each prebendal canopy has a simple cinquefoiled arch and, above, a crocketted gable of two straight sides, but with a small finial. These finials are so small that they do not require nodding ogee arches to sustain them as in the slightly later work of the Lady Chapel (III). All the way round the wall arcade there are small heads above the capitals, some of them wearing crowns, mitres, hoods or square caps. Those opposite the door all have the early form of papal mitre. The plain circular capitals of the arcade are in Blue Lias.

The magnificent central column of the room is interesting as showing the use for the first time, and that lavishly, of Purbeck Marble. Four slabs of it were laid upon the floor, and then a course of freestone to seat level. The octagonal seat itself is made up of four more slabs of marble. Above the seat is a course of freestone forming the real base of the column, and this is capped with a slab of marble, remarkable in that there are no joints in it. It is in such good condition that it looks like a restoration, but such insertion would have been impossible in one piece after the column had been built. Indeed the whole chapter house seems to have been strangely preserved considering the various purposes for which it has been used. Mr Preacher Burgess, of the Cromwellian inter-lude, tried to sell it for £160. More recently it was used as a freemason's hall and the floor is covered all over with small nails, perhaps to hold some covering. On this marble cap is built the central column of freestone with sixteen attached shafts of Purbeck Marble. The capital is either of Purbeck or Blue Lias.

The vault must be described as of a simple tierceron type although very little cross tying is used. The grand effect is obtained by the mass of ribs (32) rising from the central capital meeting those from each of the eight corners which spring from capitals supported on groups of shafts carried

Dining Hall of the College of Vicars

Corpus Christi Chapel *c.* 1330, with tombs of Dean Godelee, foreground, and Bishop Creighton

A 'Penthouse' attached to 15th century Cloisters,

The College of Vicars looking South, 14th century

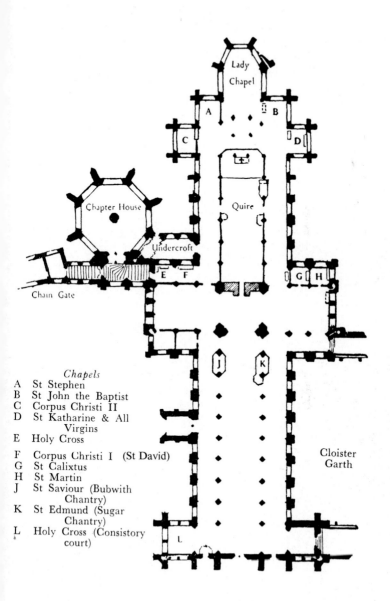

Lady
Chapel

A

B

C

D

Chapter House

Undercroft

Quire

E F

G H

Chain Gate

J

K

Cloister
Garth

Chapels

A St Stephen
B St John the Baptist
C Corpus Christi II
D St Katharine & All
      Virgins
E Holy Cross
F Corpus Christi I (St David)
G St Calixtus
H St Martin
J St Saviour (Bubwith
      Chantry)
K St Edmund (Sugar
      Chantry)
L Holy Cross (Consistory
      court)

L

The Clock. Northern face, 15th and 19th centuries

The 'Joint' of the 12th and 14th century Choirs

The Prophet Daniel, Capital in nave, discovered in 1961 above the Bubwith Chapel. 12th century. Note repair of 14th century due to tower subsidence

College of Vicars looking towards the Chapel, 14th and 15th century

Saxon Bishops' Tombs, *c.* 1235

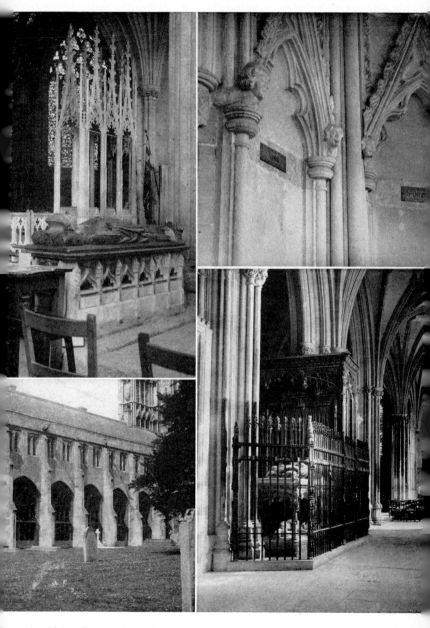

Top left: Bishop Drokensford's Tomb, 14th c.   Top right: Chapter House, 1300
Bottom left: West walk of Cloister, 15th c.   Bottom right: Bishop Beckington's Tomb.

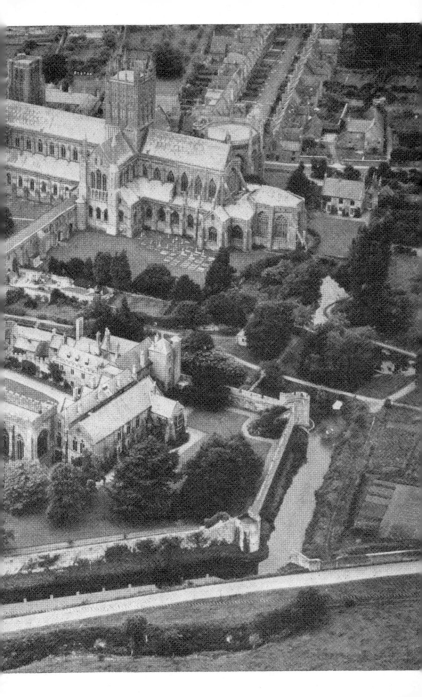

The Chain Gate, 15th century, leading from the College of Vicars to the late 13th century Chapter House Stairs

The South Eastern Chapels, 14th century

Britton: The Choir with the Throne and Old Stalls

Britton: Nave looking West, 12th century

Britton: The Lady Chapel, 14th century

Central Gable of West Front, 13th century. The statues of the Apostles are 14th century

Phillips Photo, Wells   The Annunciation. Boleyn Tomb *c.* 1470

down to bench level. There are a few relatively small bosses at the junctions. Nine ribs spread from each corner. Four rise to ribs originating at the head of each window, and the other five to another ridge rib running right round the vault. The cells of the vault are constructed of Tufa. Recent excavations at Glastonbury have shown that it was used for vaulting there. It is thought that the quarry was in the Polden Hills. We have remarked how the eight great windows resemble those of the staircase, the tracery consisting essentially of two small circles each above a pair of lights, and a large circle above again in the middle. All this is clearly *geometrical* in design, and the four main lights no longer resemble lancets. They are trefoiled right through, and above each trefoil is another, an essay in the flowing work of the mature Decorated style. Moreover there are numerous glazed piercings between the circles and the 'lancets' giving the effect of continuous tracery. Shafts have been abandoned, and the jambs of the windows consist of plain moulding with typical ball flower ornament.

At Wells we have seen that Purbeck Marble was introduced sometimes between the building of the walls and the central column of the Chapter House. We can only speculate as to the reason. It was in many ways a better and, when new, a more ornamental stone than the Blue Lias. It had, however, to be brought from the Isle of Purbeck, but improved transport was no doubt making this possible. That the marble was considered expensive is shown by the fact that in the case of two early fourteenth century tombs, the bases are still of Blue Lias, only the slab under the effigy being of thin marble.

Mention must be made of the long lines which are found traced across the floor of the Chapter House. These are scanty, and form no recognizable design whatever, and can hardly therefore be considered architectural drawings. All are straight and may well have been caused by cutting lead on the floor.

Outside the Chapter House the deep buttresses with diagonal faces rise to a group of three steps at floor level, and thence to the point where they support the main vault. Here they are nicely gabled with the same trefoil design

F

in the gable as is found in the window tracery. From them spring very fine quadrangular pinnacles, placed diagonally and rising high above the parapet. Each face is panelled in two sections with gable and finial.

The roof of the House is unique. Instead of a high pitched octagonal design as at Lincoln, it is almost flat and is built some twelve feet above the vault. The walls of the large chamber thus created are pierced by an open arcade of plain intersecting arches on a Y system. Above this again is a very open parapet of quatrefoil design and a band of dog-tooth ornament. The window labels are carried up in an ogee curve to take small finials. All this, with the undercroft standing above ground, gives exceptional height and dignity to the whole building. The curious projections from the buttresses which look like gargoyles deserve some comment. One or two figures appear to be carrying pipes but they were not connected with the roof and are much below it. It may possibly be that a roof of high pitch was intended to spring from this level and that the plan was changed as building proceeded. The almost flat existing roof is drained by what appear to be rather makeshift projecting stone pipes. It has been recently pointed out that many projections from Perpendicular Somerset church towers previously called gargoyles, are in fact purely ornamental.

THE LADY CHAPEL

We have seen that after the completion of the Chapter House, great plans were made for the extension of the east end of the cathedral. This consisted in a doubling of the length of Reginald's choir by adding three bays, the building of a new Lady Chapel (III) and the construction of a group of chapels, including two in the arms of an eastern transept.

The considerable space between the Lady Chapel and the choir is now known as the Retro-choir, although the suggestion has been made that it was intended as a feretory. Wells had no suitable saint to attract pilgrims, unlike the neighbouring abbey at Glastonbury, but there was hope and expectation that Bishop de Marcia would be canonized. The Retro-choir would have served excellently as a space for a great new shrine. It never received one, however, and we have also to remember that de Marcia already had an elaborate sepulchre in the south transept. It is now most difficult to decide the order in which the works listed above were undertaken. The documents do indeed record much expenditure during the first half of the fourteenth century, but they do not name specific objects in this connection.

A good case has been made out for the building of the Lady Chapel (III) before the other parts, so that it remained detached from the cathedral for some considerable time. The strongest evidence in favour of this consists in the jagged west ends of the building above the roof, as if buttresses previously supporting it from the west had been carelessly removed. Dean Robinson[71] discovered the names of nine canons in the glass of the chapel, and that they were all dead before 1321. He considered that the practice of the time was to erect windows during the lifetime of benefactors, and not as memorials to them. He believed that building began in the last years of the thirteenth century probably under Dean Thomas Button (1284–92), and that in any case it was completed by 1305. There was a meeting of the Chapter to confer on the fabric on April 26th, 1286, to see about 'finishing the new structure long since begun.' This, however, may refer to the Chapter House. Dean Woodforde has shown that a window in the Library may well belong to the Lady Chapel (Canon Anthony de Bradeney, †1321). There is also an inscription in the chapel in the earlier glass to Master William de Littleton, Precentor. He died in 1355. Dean Woodforde also considers on general stylistic grounds that the glass cannot be as early as the first decade of the fourteenth century.

The architectural and documentary evidence seems on balance also to be against such an early date. There is the definite statement in Drokensford's Register of 1326[72]: *a muro capellae beatae Virginis noviter constructae*. Unfortunately the window tracery, which should be our principal architectural guide, is almost unique, and cannot therefore be dated by comparison. There are two similar windows in Exeter Cathedral, being the second pair from the west in the nave. These cannot be earlier than 1330.

The Lady Chapel is an elongated octagon, and the three western sides are arches open to the Retro-choir. The remaining five sides are identical and each holds a five-light window. The main lights are boldly cinquefoiled in exactly the same way as in the great east window of the choir, except that they do not culminate in an ogee arch. The tracery is ingeniously and simply arranged. Four trefoiled openings are built on to the five lights, then three, two and one. This diminishing network pattern makes a perfect triangle, and so there are awkward gaps on each side between the chord and the arc of the two-centred window arch. These are filled in the two middle rows with distorted trefoils. There is nothing essentially 'geometrical' in all these trefoiled openings. Indeed they only need to be elongated, with the trefoil at one end, to become 'Perpendicular.' An excellent example of this may be found in the window, not far away, in the chancel of St Mary, Redcliffe. There is, however, one clear difference from the other windows of the east end, namely the absence of the ogee. It has to be remembered that this omission at least in Somerset, was characteristic of early Perpendicular work. Considered in isolation, therefore, this tracery seems to indicate a date rather towards the middle than the beginning of the fourteenth century. On the other hand, hood moulding is found outside the Lady Chapel windows and not on those of the rest of the choir. This would indicate an early date, and the undoubted break in the masonry between the chapel and the other work, shows it to *differ* in date.

It is very difficult, however, to assign other architectural detail of the chapel to the first decade of the century. Thus, apart from the entrance arches, which conform with the Retro-choir, no insets of Lias or Purbeck are to be seen. When we remember the excessive use of both in the Chapter House we can see that a new designer was here at work, belonging to a period when this sort of decoration had been given up. The fine nodding arches of the sedilia are also characteristic of a later 'Decorated' date. The piscina has vanished.

For some reason, not now apparent, the benches on each side of the chapel have been raised by a single course and a new seat provided. In the eighteenth century the Lady Chapel was used for the daily offices, and stalls were erected, so that the alteration may date from then. The mutilated reredos is probably a fifteenth century addition. Many have thought, however, that it does not belong here since the bases for the statues come so close to the floor. If it has been moved, it could only have come from the High Altar where it would have been even more out of place. Moreover, we read from the notebook of a priest-vicar[73] that the High Altar reredos was 'removed entirely away' in 1758. A new wooden cresting was designed by Sir Charles Nicholson in the 1920s, and the statue of Our Lady by A. G. Walker was erected at about the same time. High above the altar in the window jamb are some curious fittings in iron. A pair of these appear to be for lamps, and there are besides two rings. These are not in the position for hanging the Lenten Veil proper, but they may have been used for veiling the elaborate reredos in penitential seasons.

There was a building attached to the Lady Chapel on the south which was destroyed in 1822, and about which little is known. The obvious conclusion is that it was a vestry. Carter's plan shows it to have been vaulted and of considerable size, eight feet by sixteen. The front to the south was bay shaped, the centre being occupied by a door and the east face by a window. There are obvious signs of its attachment to the main building, and the present passage led into it. We should notice two curious features in connection with the room. There was a large window-like opening from it into the Lady Chapel over the bench. This was five feet broad and the marks of the filling are clear, inside and out. This opening would be more explicable if it led into a tomb rather than a vestry, but it may have been for passing out articles from a vestry instead of carrying them through the narrow passage. In this passage there is a small cupboard-like opening one foot square and rebated for a door. This has a hood roof culminating in a chimney which was carried up outside in a small lead pipe. The following suggestions as to its use have been made : (1) a lantern where a light was kept burning for use in a dark passage or to provide a flame for lighting candles, etc.; (2) an oven for baking wafers or for incinerating certain altar cloths, etc., to save them from profane use. The fact that there is no sign of the effect of heat on the stonework makes the former explanation the more likely. A small square window in the passage was glazed and also heavily barred inside the glass.

The vault of the Lady Chapel, of a lierne or star type without the peculiarities of that over the choir, is remarkably successful. The corbels are supported on triplets of plain Doulting stone rising from the bench and with a circular abacus. A main rib from each reaches to a very large central boss. This is really a medallion held by four angels. On it is carved a bearded figure of our Lord seated and in the act of blessing with both hands raised, and showing the nail marks. Other ribs rise from the corbels to meet the ridge ribs of the windows and some true liernes.

CHAPTER VI

THE CENTRAL TOWER

WHEN the Decorated builders of *c*. 1315 started to raise the central lantern on its Early English base, they took steps to reduce the size. The four main clasping buttresses at the corners were set back very slightly, but as these are recessed, the effect is more pronounced. They were then continued without a step to the top, giving an almost Perpendicular appearance to the tower. Each face was divided into three parts, bounded by four buttresses, the two outer of which adjoin those at the corners. The three panels thus created are deeply set back, involving sills sloping outwards. These formed the bases of three very tall lancet-like windows reaching upwards to the parapet of the tower. Each was divided by a central mullion so that two lancet heads were obtained. The central mullions are still *in situ,* as are the heads, now filled with elaborate later finials.

Inside, the building of the second arcade of the lantern, which had been left incomplete just above the apex of the roofs, was resumed. The arches of this are completed with a strong string course. This is considerably above the present lancet sills outside, and it seems likely that the windows up to this point were filled with masonry, as they still are. A considerable change in structure now took place. Previously, the walls had been solid and very thick, even allowing for the recesses of the lancets. Virtually two towers were erected upon this foundation, one inside the other.

The work of the outer shell was carried up without change as a framework to the lancets, except that the four face buttresses are soon brought to the end of their first stage with crocketted dormers. The inside shell of the tower consisted of a third arcade to the lantern with, like the second, three arches per side. These are really rere arches to the great outer lancets and so reach to the roof of the tower without interruption. The effect of the three arcades rising for 150 feet from the floor of the crossing must have been most impressive. (It was only seen for about twenty years before trouble began.)

The two shells of the tower coalesce at the corners in hollow buttresses, and they are frequently tied together across the intervening hollow space with ashlar blocks. It has been suggested that the inner shell was built later to strengthen the tower, but such a theory cannot be taken seriously.

Outside the top of the tower is a bold horizontal course which, with the dividing buttresses, gives square heads above the lancets. The resulting tympana are very small, and we again get the impression of a Perpendicular building. Indeed there is a remarkable resemblance between the whole tower and that of Ilminster parish church built in the late fifteenth century.

Crowning the tower is a triangular cusped open parapet which now runs round nearly the whole cathedral. Here it is thoroughly bonded with the main structure and so must date from about 1320. It was copied on many parish churches throughout Somerset for the next one hundred and fifty years.

The buttresses of this great tower are finished magnificently. Each of those at the corners has niches at the cardinal faces making eight in all. These have very high crocketted canopies over statues which stand on pillar pedestals. The whole arrangement strongly resembles that in the choir below, which is about ten years later. Considering their height, the statues are in surprisingly good condition. That on the Ws is best preserved, of St Nicholas with his left hand on the heads of the two children and his right holding a (broken) staff. The statue Wn cannot be certainly defined. The male figure is holding a square object with a central projection below. It may be a book with a marker hanging down. The figures Nw and Ne overlooking the Close are clearly of St John the Divine and St Andrew respectively. En and Es overlooking the Lady Chapel are appropriately female figures, that of Our Lady crowned, and a saint holding a martyr's palm. On the south are two bishops in full vestments, Sw being badly decayed. One is likely to be Bishop Drokensford (1309–29).

Between these statue niches the four extreme corners of the buttresses are stepped back with small pinnacles. Three of the corners of the great buttresses (the inside one remaining blank) are then carried up to end in high quadrangular sub-pinnacles. The main centre pinnacle in each corner thus appears somewhat squat. It is hexagonal and, like all the others, heavily crocketted. The two small buttresses on each face of the tower between the former lancets which, it will be remembered, were stepped back at a low level, are now capped with high pinnacles. These are only just lower than the sub-pinnacles at the corners.

The story of the subsidence of the central tower some twenty years after its erection has been dramatically told by Canon Church.[74] In 1337 the dean, Walter de London, appeals for help for the church: *fabrica ejusdem ecclesiae pro magna parte restauranda*. If the reference to restoration be taken literally, then it would seem that the tower was already giving trouble, since there can have been little else to need restoring. Next year, however, although the tower is not actually mentioned, there can be no doubt but that the reference to the fabric being *enormiter confracta et deformata*, is to the piers and other masonry of the crossing. The propping with inverted arches on north, south and west needs little comment, and the renewal of the first arches of the nave arcade, etc., has already been discussed.

The lack of an inverted arch on the east is interesting. One would expect this part to be the most vulnerable, as it was nearer the springs or wells which were causing the trouble. It may be that the very massive pulpitum, on which the organ now stands, was already in position, marking the western limit of the new choir, and that this prevented damage. On the other hand the pulpitum may have been erected after the settlement, to take the place of another inverted arch. The fact that no replacement of the choir arcade, as in the nave, was necessary makes the former explanation the more likely.

What was done in the tower itself at this time? There are cracks in the lower arcades, now above the fan vault, which have been filled with mortar, but these are not as bad as one would expect, and there is no sign here or higher up of the cutting out and replacement of masonry. Nevertheless,

the tower tilts slightly to the west. One is tempted to conjecture that its upper portion was held partly in suspension
by the powerful buttressing effect of the transepts, nave and
choir, and that the solid Early English walls really caused
the trouble. Be that as it may the damage was made good
and the tower saved. We find it again in the fifteenth century
at the crossing of Glastonbury Abbey, this time, as at Wells,
for strengthening purposes. A Victorian architect inserted a
prop, which is an exact copy of the Wells arrangement, at
Sleaford in Lincolnshire.

We find that the great lancets of the outer shell of the
tower have been filled with solid masonry in such a way as
to enhance rather than detract from its beauty. The dating
of this work has been uncertain as it seems to be rather later
in style than we would expect for 1340, when the inverted
arch props were inserted. One writer, indeed (Pevsner), puts
it as late as 1440. Dom Aelred Watkin, however, discovered a
reference in The Arundel MSS, dated May 1356, in which
the Abbot of Glastonbury concedes forty loads of stone from
his quarries at Doulting *ad reparacionem magni campanil'
ecclesie Well.'* It seems very likely that this refers to the
infilling of the lancets, and the difficulty over style is at least
partly resolved.[75] One would have expected a date even later
in the century however.

As we cannot now penetrate the solid wall backing the
two lower arcades of the lantern we do not know the position
of the sills of the earlier lancets. It is quite possible that their
lower portions were always filled with solid masonry. The
later filling, however, can be traced upwards from the top
of the second arcade inside, this being the stage at which
the tower separates into two shells. Outside, this corresponds
to a point about half way up the existing plain panel with
its trefoiled head and quatrefoil window. Above this point,
therefore, the original lancets *must* have been open.

Continuing upwards with the later filling we find that the
trefoiled head of the lower panel now supports a frieze of
quatrefoils, surmounted with a small castellated parapet, the
whole forming a substantial transom to the old lancet. The
device of a band of quatrefoils was used extensively on

fourteenth and fifteenth century Somerset church towers, often in combination with solid panelled windows. A notable example is to be found at St Cuthbert's, Wells, dated at 1440. No doubt these towers were modelled on the central tower of the mother church.

It is at this break or transom that the buttresses between the windows are stepped back with gable roofing. Immediately above, the solid masonry in each of the three lancets is pierced with a pair of small windows lighting the lantern. Between them, as between the panels below, the original mullion of 1320 remains. Strictly speaking, therefore, these openings were not lancets, as they were divided by this central mullion. Farther up again there are other castellated transoms which, however, are confined to the former lights and do not cross the window mullions. Above is another pair of small windows. All these windows have trefoiled heads, but the upper pair has a shallow outer arch as well, which is cinquefoiled. Next, and fitting between the upper pair almost like plate tracery, is a large quatrefoil. Finally, there is a shallow canopy of straight crocketted sides with, at its apex, a finial so large that it quite fills the head of the light of the former lancet.

All this insertion work can be quite easily followed from the inside, but it might be as well to record that there was extensive renewal of the finial area about 1913 and that the modern work has been bonded in with that of 1320 to give greater strength, but destroying in places all evidence of the filling.

So far we have considered the strengthening of the outer tower shell. What of the inner? The first two blank arcades from the crossing, with the immensely thick wall behind, have not been disturbed. We have already mentioned that the inner shell contained rere arches to the tall lancets. They were of great height and were obviously considered to be a source of weakness, although there is no sign that the masonry gave way or cracked. The lower portions of these rere arch openings have been filled with massive grid-like masonry. This has two openings to each lancet. As the lower is the larger, the effect is of a late Tudor window. We have no evidence when this work was done except that it is well finished, with chamfered edges and so, presumably, was at one time visible from the floor of the crossing. It would thus be earlier than the fan vault which cuts off the lantern. On the top of this filling a wooden floor has been placed. The main timbers are very old, and may date from 1338. In a print of the time of Dean Brailsford (1713–33) and in others by Simes (1735) and Buck in the same year, together with an oil painting by Henry de Cort about 1795, a large centre turret is shown to the tower which must have changed its appearance considerably during the 18th century. It had disappeared from the drawings of Britton (1822). As far as its design can be made out from these rather unsatisfactory sources it would appear to date from the 17th century and may have been part of the restoration work of Dean Creyghton (1660–1674), and to have housed the great hour bell of the clock. The present bell is modern and is in one of the corner turrets.

CHAPTER VII

THE WEST FRONT AND TOWERS

WE have seen that the last three bays of the nave were building from 1220–30. In the absence of direct documentary
evidence, the later date is the best that can be suggested for
the lay-out of the front. It is supported by Robinson and
Bilson and, more recently, by Lawrence Stone. The accepted
date for the completion of the front has been 1239, according to the charter of Bishop Jocelin in which he says that he
'dedicated the church' in November of that year : *Noveritis
nos in dedicatione ecclesiae nostrae Wellensis quam die sancti
Romani mense Novembris anno incarnationis dominicae 1239
in honorem sancti Andreae apostolorum mitissimi dedi-
cavimus. . . .*[76] Critical examination of the sculpture, however, seems to show that some of it may not have been
completed for another ten years.

In a charter issued in the year of his death, 1242,[77] the
bishop grants increased emoluments to all the cathedral clergy
and says he does so because the church is now completed,
furnished with all things necessary and consecrated anew.
The most likely explanation seems to be that the front was
built sufficiently high to close the nave by 1239. The fact
that all the statues save one are detached, shows that they
could have been added subsequently over quite a long period,
even though some form of scaffolding would have to remain
or be re-erected. Doubt has been expressed as to whether
the western gable had in fact been closed by the time of
the dedication in 1242, but Robinson was clearly of the
opinion that it had, since he says 'The statement may well
mean that all inside work was properly finished off; but it
leaves us quite free to suppose that the external ornamentation of the West Front was still being carried forward.'

The plan of this magnificent screen of sculpture is simple
enough. Its width of 148 feet is divided into five unequal
divisions by six enormous buttresses. Two of these in the
centre form the abutment to the nave arcades. They are

surmounted by gables and heavy hexagonal pinnacles, surrounded by detached shafts with circular capitals and waterholding bases. Two pairs of buttresses, north and south, provide a normal abutment to the towers. These six, of course, face west. Two others, their sides covered with statues, support the towers at each end, and serve to increase the width of the great façade. Between the corner buttresses diagonal surfaces of the towers are exposed, and behind, concealed in the thickness of the masonry, rise the newel stairs. Two more buttresses support the towers at their rear corners. These meet exactly at right angles since there are no stairs. At the north end of the front, sculpture is continued right round until the nave wall is reached on the east side.

Who was responsible for this plan and what were his intentions for its completion? The most likely person seems to be Elias de Dereham (1188–1245). He was a canon of Wells and Salisbury, and was known to be responsible for building work at the latter cathedral from 1220–45. He was a friend of the two brother bishops from Wells, Jocelin and Hugh.[78] The master mason, Adam Lock, died at this time, 1229. He probably completed the nave under the direction of Dereham, who was known to him and witnessed a deed disposing of some of his private property. He was succeeded at Wells by Thomas Norreys (1229–49), who would thus be in charge of the building of the front.[79]

There are three tiers of statues on the west front, and two more in the central gable. A satisfactory sense of solidity is afforded by a deep plinth matching that of the earlier work in the nave, and then, rising to the top of the aisle doors, absolutely plain masonry. This is in remarkably good condition and appears not to have been anywhere restored. Cut in it on the front face of the buttress by the north-west door is an interesting inscription in Lombardic letters[80] : *PVR LALME IOHAN DE PUTTENIE PRIEZ ET TREZE IVRS DE*. Canon Christopher Wordsworth of Salisbury suggested the addition of the words *pardon averez* to make a rhyming couplet after the fashion of the time : 'For the soul of John de Pitney pray, and receive thirteen days indulgence.' It is thought that this is a memorial to a John of

Pitney, a priest who held several benefices in the diocese, and who probably died in the plague in 1348. If so, the unfinished inscription may indicate that the mason also fell a victim to the pestilence. As his memorial faces the churchyard, John of Pitney is probably buried not far away.

Besides the small aisle entrances, contrived as it were in the plinth of the front, the central doorway is carried to twice the height. It still remains tiny compared with the vast portals of French cathedrals of this date. This central door has a trumeau and, in the resulting large tympanum, a quatrefoil containing a much mutilated seated figure of Our Lady and Child, with large censing angels on each side. The arch is of four orders and three of them carry the usual plain Early English rolls with fillets. The first order is, however, remarkable since each voussoir has a flower of square shape occupying most of its face. In the centres of some are shown seeds or fruit like tiny bunches of grapes. The carving is very fine and is deeply undercut. It appears to be much later than other work on the west front and has been used as an argument for a date as late as 1260 for the whole building. In fact, however, this date would be too early for such carving which may belong to the next century. It cannot have been inserted, being an integral part of the arch. It is possible, if not probable, that it was carved *in situ* out of a plainer arch. In the two large hollows another curious thing has happened. Carving has been inserted round the arch in a stone, White Lias, found nowhere else in the cathedral. The first hollow is filled with conventional foliage, but the second consists of a row of niches with canopies resembling others on the front. In each is the figure of an angel, but all are decapitated. Thus there has been a general attempt to 'improve' the appearance of this doorway by adding ornament at subsequent dates.

In the jamb of the doorway, about five feet from the ground, is a nice example of a pilgrim's cross : these are often wrongly called consecration crosses. Perched on the apex of the doorway arch is a wide cinquefoiled niche with a gable top. This contains the two seated figures, now decapitated, of the Coronation of Our Lady. The wall behind is regularly peppered with small holes, popularly supposed to have been caused by bullets aimed at the statues. Actually many of these are filled with wood, and probably served to hold metallic stars of a background sky. Ferrey stated that when examined with scaffolding in 1873 the figure of Our Lord at the apex of the high gable above showed bullet marks.

The gable top of the Coronation niche just reaches the bold string course which divides the front into two parts at rather below the half-way mark. Statues of the first tier occupying this space are arranged in replicas of the central doorway, i.e. in pairs on each side of a 'trumeau,' with projecting gables and quatrefoils over containing figures of angels. Eight of these spaces, however, serve as windows, later filled with Perpendicular tracery, to light the nave aisles and bases of the towers. The shafts used to frame the niches over the whole front were formerly of Blue Lias and a few of this stone remain in the doorways. During the extensive restoration by Ferrey in 1867 the greater number were replaced by Kilkenny marble. This was much criticized at the time, but the harsh colour has weathered in the intervening century, and they are still in perfect condition. Except round the north-west tower the statues of this lower tier have perished. It is not known whether they were pulled down at the Reformation, the Cromwellian usurpation, or the Monmouth rebellion, those three crises in the history of the building. Each pair of niches of the first tier is surmounted with a bold straight gable giving an overall zig-zag effect. In the resulting tympana are quatrefoils containing scriptural scenes, Old Testament on the south and New Testament on the north.

We have now reached the first step of the great buttresses which display most of the sculpture. As a result of the set back, their faces have room for only one statue instead of a pair, although their sides retain two. None however are arranged in pairs, so there are now no large gables and resulting quatrefoils. These two tiers of statues are therefore architecturally much less prominent than the first tier. This is as it should be, or a top-heavy effect would have resulted. The second main horizontal division of the front really consists of great lancets, some glazed, some blank, some filled with statues. In the central division between the arcade buttresses are three main lancets, glazed and forming the great west window of the nave. They are bounded by four smaller lancets of statues. On each side of the central buttresses are pairs of blank lancets, their heads filled with foliage and with small slit windows which light the triforium space behind.

The plain filling is here undoubtedly part of the Early English building. We cannot be so certain about the next pair on each side of the tower buttresses, and now forming the main faces of the towers. Indeed it seems likely that this filling was inserted in Perpendicular days when the towers above were built, and that open unglazed spaces were originally intended. The masonry is not bonded in; the heads are not filled, like all the others, with carving; the small windows are trefoiled and must be later. Moreover the high chambers behind, which reach right from the vaults of the rooms in the bases of the towers to the top of the Early English work, are curiously well finished, as if they would be exposed to view. A bench is provided, and from it rise shafts on three of the four sides. On the east side the shafts rise from a carved corbel. These support the first tas-de-charge courses of vaults which were never built. A curious feature of the chamber in the southern tower is a heavy course of ancient timber let into the walls just above bench level. This may have provided a temporary roof to what was then a porch entrance to the church under the tower. It is about the right distance above the vault. No such arrangement appears in the northern tower.

The points of each of this great row of lancets across the entire front reach to the bases of a new and relatively small series of trefoiled openings. These form the 'Resurrection Tier,' filled with groups of statuary showing the naked dead arising from stone tombs.[81] Above is a strong string course and here, except for the central gable, the Early English front ends. We have no inkling as to the sort of towers the thirteenth century builders intended to use to crown their front, nor whether they were to have steeples. Although

G

building did not proceed to the north and south, it was very necessary to raise the central gable in order to close the end of the nave. This was probably done in time for the dedication by Bishop Jocelin in 1239. The only two buttresses carried up beyond this point, to flank the central gable, are those providing abutment to the main arcades. It was desirable therefore to finish them. They are not set back at this stage, thus conforming with the usual Early English type, which had few steps or none at all. Soon however they were crowned with their pinnacles to give the necessary weight.

Across the space between the now blank cinquefoiled niches of the last stage of these buttresses are nine similar but smaller openings. These contain figures of the nine orders of the heavenly company : Throne, Cherub, Seraph, Power, Virtue, Domination, Principality, Archangel, and Angel. Above, between the bases of the pinnacles, are the twelve apostles in narrower but much higher trefoiled niches. They are arranged in sets of three divided by an extra shaft of lias. Some still carry their symbols with SS Andrew and John in the centre. They are, however, totally different from other statuary of the front, stand on pedestals, and must be dated well on in the fourteenth century. It is difficult to explain this late date since the work above them is thirteenth century. One would not have expected this important feature to have been left blank in the first place, nor a renewal after so short a period. Above the apostles we come to the crowning feature of the gable, which just closes the apex of the nave roof behind. A large oval opening (ten cusped) still holds the legs of a draped and seated figure. Undoubtedly this was a Christ in Majesty. The smaller trefoiled openings, one on each side, formerly held figures, probably of censing angels. There seems originally to have been a row of cross-like finials on the top of this feature, but it is unlikely that they have survived in this exposed position. In the centre there is now a large octagonal pinnacle of the same date as the apostles. No doubt it was put in position at the same time.

So the front was left for 150 years without its flanking

towers. One reason for this apparent neglect seems to be that the authorities considered the provision of the Chapter House and enlarged Choir to be more important. There must also have been an early decision to alter the whole external balance of the church since a central tower was built to a height of 165 feet. This meant that the western towers must now be subordinate to it, and relatively unimportant. The Early English builders intended the reverse, i.e. high western towers, probably with steeples, and a low central lantern.

Bishop Harewell, died 1386, gave money towards the building of the south-west tower.[82] The cathedral Master Mason at this time was William Wynford (1365–1405). In his contract with the Dean and Chapter he swore 'to be their good and faithful servitor for the term of his life and to oversee the fabric and the workmen engaged thereon,' all this for an annual salary of £2 and 6d. a day. No specific documents connect him with the tower, but he must have supervised its erection. To what extent, if at all, he was responsible for its design we cannot know. The name 'lathamus' would seem to indicate an actual worker in stone, and is used in the cathedral accounts to describe casual contractors, like the man who did some paving in the cloisters.[83] Probably these medieval 'architects' occupied a position which to-day would be intermediate between the designer and the worker.

There are two schools of thought about the design of these towers. One maintains that there was little scope for imagination since the plan, including the size of the buttresses, was fixed; and that all the later builder had to do was to continue in the early Perpendicular idiom of his time. The other considers that only a genius could have put a Perpendicular tower on an Early English base. The reader must take his choice, although few would deny that the operation was eminently successful.

Except for the plan, the new architect paid little attention to the older work below. He continued the buttresses upward with a small set-back. Gone, however, are the statues, shafts, canopies and foliage carving of the thirteenth century, and plain panelling is substituted. The essential feature of these Perpendicular towers at Wells is the pair of two light 'windows.' Below a transom, thin panels of masonry take the place of wooden louvres.

They undoubtedly set the fashion for this sort of tower in the county, and were copied at Evercreech, Wrington and Wells (St Cuthbert's) and to a lesser degree elsewhere.[84]

The set-back of the Perpendicular work of the towers, particularly in the panels of the windows, involved long blank sloping surfaces; but these have been relieved by ridges giving a roof-like appearance. This device had in fact been copied from the adjoining pinnacles of the gable, and thus a valuable degree of continuity is obtained. The two windows are separated from each other by a shaft or buttress which rises right from the Early English work to the top of the parapet. In contrast with the central tower however there are no pinnacles on it or on the corner buttresses. The windows themselves are of simple design. The panels below the transom are trefoiled and provided with small window slits. They are of very thin masonry, and so a relieving arch has been built to support the heavy castellated transom. This arch is visible from the front in all the eight windows of each tower, and has led to the unlikely suggestion that it formerly covered a glazed opening or window proper.

The upper parts above the transom, containing wooden louvres, have trefoiled main lights and a simple central six-foiled opening for tracery. This is of a very common pattern found all over England, for example in Westminster Hall (1397). A heavy string course touches the apexes of both windows, and meets the buttresses on each side. This gives a panel-like effect, leaving tympana which are carved out almost in Tudor fashion.

Above is a blank trefoiled panelled parapet and final castellation, 125 feet from the ground.

It is however in the arrangement of the buttresses that the designer has shown his skill : in other respects the towers are conventional enough. Set back somewhat at the base of the Perpendicular work, they are very abruptly carried inwards about two-thirds of the way up thus giving the towers their rather squat appearance. In front the buttresses have simple trefoiled panels, which become double at the sides.

At the main set-back they are provided with gables and pinnacles. A sloping roof then carries them back to smaller buttresses set in pairs diagonally at each corner of the tower. The outer pairs, however, are filled in, and tend to lose their shape since they are made to carry stairs. Between each of the inner pairs the corners of the towers may be seen and the same arrangement holds for the diagonally opposite corners at the rear. There are no buttresses at the inner rear corners. The smaller diagonal buttresses have two courses of the inevitable trefoiled panels. This carries them right up to the castellation at the summit, preserving their individuality, since they have no connection with the small parapet over the windows. On neither tower is there any sign of a steeple.

The north-west tower was built during the episcopate of Bishop Stafford (1425–43), with funds left by his predecessor, Bubwith, †1424. Bubwith directed that the tower should be a duplicate of that on the south-west, and that it should not be begun until the library, which he also provided, was finished.[85] The differences between the two towers are in fact trivial, except that canopies containing statues were fixed on the faces of the two main buttresses. That to the north still contains the kneeling figure of Bubwith in cope, mitre and staff, with his restored arms below. His arms are also to be found on a shield at the rear of the tower. The niche on the southernmost buttress is vacant, but traditionally contained a statue of Bishop Stafford who was translated to Canterbury in 1443. His restored arms appear below.

On a print dedicated to Dean Brailsford (mid-eighteenth century) a wall, capped with parapet, is shown joining the two tower buttresses on the ground. Other prints show railings. In the same print a curious canopy may be seen attached to the stonework by the north-west door. Traces of this having been secured by iron stays remain.

CHAPTER VIII

THE CLOISTERS

THE cloisters at Wells, as in other secular cathedrals like Salisbury, were probably built partly for reasons of prestige, copying those of monastic establishments, rather than for use. They also provided an undercroft for rooms on the first floor according to the custom of early fifteenth century domestic building. There is no sign at Wells of such offices as a lavabo, nor does the Chapter House lead out of them as in the great Benedictine churches. Also, there is no north walk. The three massive outer walls built in random courses of local stone are of a much earlier date. They probably supported earlier cloisters.

Bishop Bubwith in his will dated October 5th, 1424,[86] left 1,000 marks 'to be faithfully applied and disposed for the construction and new building of a certain library to be newly erected upon the eastern space or part of the cloister of the said church of Wells, situate between the southern door of the said church next the Chamber of the Eschaetor of the same church, and the gate which leads directly from the church by the cloister aforesaid into the episcopal palace.' Here we have reference to a former cloister, although it is clear that the inner walls were now entirely rebuilt. Work must have begun after 1424. Fourteen bays were laid out for the East walk between the two doors mentioned, both of which still exist. One bay of the southern walk, turning the corner, also belongs to this time. The bays consist of a large window or screen towards the garth, with buttresses to support the vault and upper storey. There is no wall on this side.

The vault is of a fairly complex lierne type springing from the four corners of the cell. There is merely an indication of a capital so that the ribs appear to rise from bench level. Above the capital, however, are trefoiled panels which really support the ribs. In these panels we may see the beginning of the fan vault, although this had been well developed else-

where, particularly at Gloucester Abbey long before. Wells
was thus very old-fashioned in this construction of its cloisters.

Above the screen on the garth side is a fair space of blank
wall, and in each division a pair of two-light, trefoiled, square-
headed windows for the library. Some of these have been
blocked with modern brickwork. Surmounting all is a plain
parapet with gargoyles over every other buttress. The roof
was of lead with a low pitch, and the modern high pitched
slated type must have changed the appearance considerably.
The bay nearest the cathedral is of an odd size, rather less
than half the others. The lower portion of its screen provides
a door to the garth. The layout of this east walk was not
quite accurate, as it had to be set back two inches when
it neared the southern corner. This may be seen on the
parapet. Inside there is no bench towards the garth as there
is on the outer side. In the southern and eastern walks, however, we find a heavy roll at bench height.

Between the third and fifth buttresses were two doorways,
now blocked, contrived in the screenwork. These lead out
into the two very curious penthouses built between the buttresses. They seem to be contemporary with the rest of the
building and each is divided by a pillar giving four centred
low arched openings to the west. Their purpose remains
obscure, and no similar works are found in other secular
cloisters. At Gloucester each bay of the monastic cloister has
a carel, or retiring recess, where monks could read or
meditate. These, however, are part of the cloister and protected from the weather, whereas at Wells they are outside
and open. Also there are no signs of seats. At Glastonbury
the foundations of two such penthouses were found outside
a cloister of much the same date, and facing the chapter
house entrance. Here at Wells they faced the entrance to
the old Lady Chapel, *juxta claustrum*.

One suggestion is that the penthouses covered tombs, but
there are no signs of monumental attachments to the walls,
and tentative excavations recently carried out revealed no
burials. In the spandrils of the arch of one of the penthouses
were two attached carved initials, of which only one, N or R,
remains. It is idle to speculate as to the owner of these, but

the two letters may have been N.B., for Nicholas Bubwith.

For the section nearest the church, the old eastern cloister wall was retained only up to the height of the library floor. Here we must note that the library room and perhaps the cloister below was built in two stages. The only sign of this on the garth side is that one of the buttresses, the seventh, is considerably wider than the others and may have marked a temporary end. On the east, however, towards the church-yard known as the Camery, there are other signs of a break. These are, incidentally, now marked, and to an extent masked, by a privy of uncertain date approached from the library and standing out from the wall like a tower. Between this point and the church, the old cloister wall was pulled down to the floor level of the library and a new thinner wall was built on it. This gave greater width for the room which was lit from the west with square-headed windows as on the garth side, although they are now much obscured by the later work for Stillington's chapel.

There were, and still are, buttresses against the Early English wall but they do not correspond to the bays of the new cloister, and so cannot take the thrust of the vault. The builders therefore inserted large blocks of ashlar into the top of the lowered wall opposite each capital of the vault, so that the thrust might be taken. These blocks, in sets of three, are clearly visible from the camery. Buckle[87] considers that these are the sawn off corbels of a penthouse roof, and he takes the projecting window sills above to be a weather-course. It seems unlikely, however, that any one would take the trouble to saw the stones off so carefully and the sill or weathercourse also varies in height. Anyway, above these blocks a thin ashlar wall has been built for the library. This was the method adopted down to the privy or break. It is suggested that funds now became short so that the whole height of the old thick wall was then used above floor level. This has meant a considerable narrowing of the library room. It was not easy, or perhaps unnecessary, to insert the ballast blocks in the massive old wall to take the vault thrust. Also windows on this side were omitted, the existing ones having been inserted in the seventeenth century, perhaps at the expense of the then Treasurer, Dr Busby (†1695).

On the gable end of the library over the bishops' door are the arms of Bubwith, the original benefactor. This either means that the room was completed, using the funds of his legacy, or that the shield was removed from a temporary end at the break. Work on the cloister below was evidently not completed until 1458, long after Bubwith's death. The Fabric Roll for 1457–8 records payment to John Turpyn, Mason (*lathamo*) of £6 11s. 3d. or three farthings a foot for paving fourteen bays.[88]

We have seen that the first bay of the south walk was completed with this work, the corner being turned, but the joint is very clumsily made on the window side. This is due to the fact that the wall of the south walk was made thinner and so the exterior window splays do not correspond. A single mullion separates the windows where they join at right-angles. The cloister screen has been copied all the way round, although there is considerable difference in date. Each unit is of an orthodox Perpendicular design (the ogee curve is missing) of the mid-fifteenth century, having six lights, the centre mullion being larger than the others and dividing into the familiar Y form to reach the main two-centred arch. Thus two windows are virtually formed. Above them, and between the arms of the Y, is a large panel, cinquefoiled top and bottom. The spaces on both sides of it are filled with regular quatrefoils in circular frames. Each three lights of the sub unit is surmounted by two tracery panels, also cinquefoiled top and bottom, and above again carry an irregular quatrefoil. The lower part of the arcade has a very heavy transom which visually, and no doubt structurally, ties the buttresses together. The main lights are cinquefoiled at their heads and at the transom.

None of the lights now has glass, but provision is made by the usual slit for glazing above the transom in the east walk, as well as for two lights below it opposite the Stilling ton door. No sign of glass or lead has ever been discovered, and there is no provision for glazing in the west walk. On the south, only the cusped portions of the tracery lights have slits.

There are some curious unexplained features by the door-way leading to the Camery Churchyard, and formerly into the Stillington Chapel. On the south side the bench has been cut away as if to make another door out of the cloister, but there is no disturbance of the wall itself. Above are two longitudinal panels framed with plain fifteenth century mould-ing as if made for pictures. At the southern top of the upper panel is a bracket which may have held a small statue or light. Above again is a carving in stone (low relief) of some of the symbols of the passion. It is rapidly decaying but the scourge and spear are still clearly visible. Under the vault may be seen the imprint of the Ascension panel now removed to Corpus Christi (II) Chapel.

The West Walk of the Cloister was the next to be built, and like that on the east it included one bay of the southern division. There is also a short bay next the church, but it is clear that the masons were incapable of doing the necessary arithmetic involved in the set out, since they arrived at the far end with a foot to spare, which has been incorporated in the most clumsy fashion into the last window, resulting in a nearly circular arch. Here again, as on the east side, the Early English wall has been used. This would seem to be of the time of Jocelin since it is bonded into the West Front, and in the seventh bay there are remains of a large door-way with capitals of this period. It is possible that this formed the lay-people's entrance to the church via the South-West Tower, as there are indications of a porch out-side built into later buildings.

There is no documentary evidence as to the date of this walk but the vault contains the arms of Bishop Beckington, †1465. Like the east walk, there was an upper storey made into several rooms for the song school and other purposes. To supplement this accommodation some rooms of doubtful date, but possibly fifteenth century, have been built out into the garden of the organist's house which is now in ruins. A room with a separate staircase coming down into the eighth bay has been traditionally used by the cathedral glaziers.

The same archaic vaulting of the cloister is continued except that the liernes are linked to square panels at the centre of each bay. These and the bosses have carvings of considerable interest which we will now consider.

PANEL I, counting from the Cathedral door, contains the arms of Bishop Beckington (1443–65), (*Arg*) *on a fess* (*Az*), *betw. in chief three bucks' heads caboshed* (*gu.*) *and in base as many pheons* (*sa.*) *a bishop's mitre* (*or*). On one of the bosses of this bay we find again the three pheons alone. These formed the arms of Nicholl, a Welsh family. A William Nicholl was vicar of Woolavington in 1452 and died in 1480.[89] On a boss in the thirteenth bay are the three bucks' heads alone : these were for Bowett. Henry Bowett was Bishop of Bath and Wells 1401–7. Thus it is apparent that Beckington, of a weaver's family from a place of that name near Frome, used the arms of these two families, adding a mitre in the centre. A Nicholl and a Bowett may have been his friends.

PANEL II has the Beckington rebus, a fire beacon lit, the vessel containing the fire being a tun or barrel. Bosses in this bay display a horned man and a winged animal.

PANEL III has again Beckington's arms, and bosses with two dogs and a quadruped with human head.

PANEL IV has the bishop's initials T.B., but one of the bosses contains an interesting shield held by an angel. The arms on it are for Witham, *a bend between three eagles closed*. William Witham was Dean of Wells (1464–72).

In PANEL V the rebus is repeated, and is a beautiful piece of work in great detail. Supporting bosses are of two dragons, a man carrying two staves, a bird, a strange animal and two men's faces in foliage.

PANEL VI again has the arms of the bishop, with bosses of the face of a bird in foliage, and another of a large bird.

PANEL VII has the rebus. Bosses are of a naked man, two men with musical instruments (these are over the door leading to the song school), a boy climbing, and a strange animal.

PANEL VIII has the Beckington arms.

In PANEL IX is the figure of a bird forming the letter T. Supporting bosses are of a man's face in foliage, and two men.

PANEL X has the initial letter B, so that adjoining bays make up T.B. for Thomas Beckington. A man's trunk is visible on one of the bosses.

PANEL XI repeats once more the Beckington rebus. On one of the bosses are three tiny human figures and a shield; on another, Dean Witham's arms are given for a second time.

On PANEL XII there is the large initial T, and all the bosses have figures, a man with a peculiar instrument, four swans, probably for Swan, one of Beckington's executors, a tonsured head, a devil with horns and tail, a dog, a bearded head.

PANEL XIII has the arms again; and one of the bosses contains those of Bowett mentioned under the first bay, i.e. three bucks' heads caboshed. Another has a man, a third two men holding a staff, and a fourth the rebus.

PANEL XIV and the bay form the corner containing the monument to Bishop Hooper. The rebus is repeated and the main work and bosses are without interest.

PANEL XV and its bay are round the corner in the south walk, and this ends the Beckington work. It will be remembered that the Bubwith or east walk was also continued one bay round the S.E. corner. For some time the south walk thus had only a bay at each end and there was a gap of twelve bays. This last Beckington bay has the bishop's arms in the panel, and those of Chancellor Sugar, an executor, on a boss. These are three sugar loaves, and in chief a doctor's cap. A bird may represent the other executor Swan, and on three bosses are angels apparently holding symbols of the passion.

For the south walk, Bishop Stillington, 1466–91, may have provided some funds, since his arms are included. The work, however, was not begun until some sixteen years after his death, and was the last piece of medieval building to be undertaken in the cathedral. The windows were exactly copied from the earlier works, but the vault was modified.

The ribs now spring directly from a small foliated capital and not from a fan panel. The crown is eight inches higher but the difference is hardly noticeable. The outside south wall was, as before, the old work of the thirteenth century. Its heavy buttresses are similar to those in Bishop Jocelin's palace, and there is a doorway, 'the bishop's door' of this date in the south-east corner. This door now opens, as one would expect, inwards but it once opened outwards and the rehanging has involved some destruction of carving.

The reason for this alteration seems to be fairly clear. In the thirteenth century, before the digging of the moat or erection of the palace fortifications, this area south of the cloisters was simply the bishop's private garden, and so the door opened outwards into it from the cloisters. In the same bay at this corner there is another Early English doorway the remains of which can be seen outside, now opening into the mason's yard. This may have been used for processions round the church.

Leland (c. 1550) has this to say, 'Beckington began also the south side of the cloister, but Thomas Henry or Harryes, Treasurer of Welles and Archidiacon of Cornewaull made an ende of it in hominum memoria. This side has no housing over it.'[90] All symbols of this bishop cease abruptly at the break but we do find memorials to Bishop Stillington. It happens that we know more about the economics of this cloister building than any other part of the church. The cathedral accounts show that the work was newly begun in 1507, and that Henry the Treasurer paid for the stone work and 'wages of masons,' whereas the canons residentiary provided the rest, such as timber and lead, 'at the expense of the church goods.'[91]

The vault carvings of the south walk are very fine, but they have suffered considerable damage, and are still encrusted with whitewash and dirt. It is known that the prisoners after Sedgemoor were confined in the cloisters and it may have been in this section only.[92] Damage, apparently due to the erection of partitions or fences, may be traced in the south-west corner. Significantly, boys of the Grammar School were forbidden to play in the cloister in 1606.[93] We also learn that in 1725 James Bacon, Junior Clerk, is forbidden to keep horses or sheep in the Palm Churchyard or to allow them to come into the church or cloisters. It is not improbable that this part of the cloister was used, particularly during the Commonwealth, for general farming and storage purposes. There are indications that an iron bar was fixed across all the windows about half way up to the transom. This may have served to keep animals in the churchyard or garth, but it would not have prevented a man from climbing through.

Continuing with a consideration of the carvings in the vault, we find in Bay XVI, the first after the break, a good representation of Bishop Stillington's arm in the main panel. These are *a chevron between three leopards' faces*. The bishop had been dead some sixteen years. Henry, however, was appointed his Vicar General in the last year of his life. This was an important office in days when the bishops were almost entirely absent from their dioceses. When Fox succeeded in 1492, he did not continue Henry in this office, and there is no reference to this bishop in the carvings of the gap. The bay also contains a shield, now indecipherable, and another in a bad state, but with the letters T.H. (Thomas Henry) still visible on it. Panel XVII has a large Tudor rose and, on the bosses, a man with cloak and sword, and a bird.

PANEL XVIII has the first examples of the beautiful figures of angels characteristic of this section. There are four on the panel stretched out facing the floor with their feet together in the centre, giving a wheel effect. They are in girdled albs and here carry a text on a bannerette which goes round the panel. This cannot now be deciphered. In the same bay the bosses have the figure of a man, the letter T, four owls and two dogs.

PANEL XIX. The arms of the deanery are supported by two angels, and the bosses have a letter medallion T.H. and an owl.

PANEL XX has a fine Tudor Royal Arms held by four angels as in Bay XVIII, their bodies hidden by the shield. They carry a bannerette with *Hony soyt que malle pense*. A subsidiary boss has the usual set of four angels holding the arms of the see and a T.H. Another boss has the letter H alone.

PANEL XXI. Again the four angels bear an arms. This time it is of Daubeney; *four fusils conjoined in fesse* and is surrounded by the Garter as in the last bay. This would belong to Giles, Lord Daubeney, K.G. He died in 1508 and is buried at Westminster. The same arms without the garter are found in the window of St Calixtus' Chapel and are probably those of his father, William Daubeney of South Petherton (†1460). Lord Daubeney, who held many offices under the Crown, was made steward of the bishop in 1493, and of the dean and chapter in 1503.[94] He may have contributed to the cost of the cloister, or been a patron of Henry.

William Worcester, writing of Wells about 1480, says that: 'there are three cloisters, arched and vaulted, and in each of the three, twelve great windows.'[95] This is curious in the face of evidence that the south cloister was not begun before 1507, but it may have been laid out sufficiently for the bays to be counted.

PANEL XXII has the arms of Stillington repeated, held by the four angels, and in a fine state of preservation. A boss has the arms of the deanery *a saltire between two keys addorsed, the bows interlaced, on the dexter, and a sword erect on the sinister*. Another boss contains four human heads.

PANEL XXIII. Two angels are on the centre panel holding a much mutilated and indecipherable text.

PANEL XXIV. In the last bay the four angels are once more holding a text, alas, like some of the others, too damaged and dirty to read.

In 1509 a sleeping chamber was granted to one John Pety in the cloisters.[96] This doubtless was one of several possible rooms over the west walk. Another room below is mentioned in 1741 when Charles Prowse, Chapter Clerk, collects records into 'the ground room in the cloisters, near the door at the entrance to the audit room.'[97] Both these rooms can be identified with some certainty since there is only one chamber on the ground, although it does not appear very suitable for records. A room above, now approached by a wooden stairs, had a grand doorway given to it in the eighteenth century, and was made more comfortable in Regency times. No doubt it was used for audits. An audit room is mentioned in 1372 as being over a gate on the west side of the cloister.[93] This of course could not have been part of the present range of buildings.

Leland refers definitely to two chapels in connection with the cloisters, both of which have utterly disappeared : *Nicholas Bubbewith . . . fecit panellam Claustri cum capella inferius et libraria superius.* There is no other reference to this chapel and it seems impossible to suggest a place for it actually under the library. The only possible site would be that of the curious small building which jutted out eastwards into the Camery from the second bay of Bubwith's cloister, the screen or window of which may be seen from the outside. Leland also says 'There is no part of the cloister . . . on the north side of the area to walk in, for it is only hemmid with the South isle of the body of the chirch. There is only a chapel in that side of the area made by one Cukeham.' No doubt this latter chapel existed, since references to it are numerous, and the only possible conclusion seems to be that it was a separate building in the northern portion of the garth. No scars are visible to show attachment to the nave aisle, and the ground has been so buried over that the possibility of finding foundations is remote. This 'Cookham's chapel' was dedicated to All Saints and the first reference to it is in 1348 when Alice Swansee desired to be buried opposite the chapel of All Saints by the cloister near her son Phillip Swansee, late vicar.[99] It seems that the vicars had right of burial in the Palm Churchyard or garth, and the canons in the cloister itself. The name Cookham became attached to the chapel after 1384, when Canon William Cookham left money for a recitation of the office of the dead.[100]

Members of the College of Annuellar Priests, established in what is now the North Liberty in the early fifteenth century, were also buried in and around All Saints' Chapel.[101] Orders in medieval days were given quietly to individuals, usually in a side chapel without the pomp and ceremony associated with the modern service, and nearly always by a suffragan bishop. Nevertheless a reasonable space was obviously required, and we can assume that as they were conferred in Cookham's chapel, this was a building of some size. Thus in 1461, the Bishop of Tenos (suffragan to Beckington) ordained an acolyte, Richard ap Eynon of St David's in 'Cokains Chapel.'[102] On May 17th, 1480, Master Thomas Fortt, M.A., was instituted to the Vicarage of Yeovil in the chapel of All Saints in the Palm Churchyard.[103]

The earlier cloisters may have been of wood leaning against the old outer wall still remaining. On the other hand various bits of Early English carving built into a later chapel in the Vicars' Close and Mellifont 'Abbey,' Wookey, came traditionally, although there seems no evidence, from these early cloisters.

The library chamber over Bubwith's cloister was 165 feet long, and we cannot tell how it was furnished and used in medieval times. As reconstructed after the troubles of the seventeenth century there seems to have been a room, as at present, about seventeen feet square overlooking the palace. The library proper stretched from this for some sixty feet towards the cathedral and was divided off by a partition, just north of the entrance to the external privy. About half the whole space was thus left unused. Then in 1728 there was an extension of thirty-three feet and the partition was moved northwards to its present position. This was to accommodate the books left to the library by Bishop Hooper, and it seems likely that the whole was panelled at this time.[104] £65 5s. 5d. was paid to Thomas Parfitt in 1728 for this purpose and the panelling is the same as in his own house in the town which dates at c. 1730. The bookcases may be of this date or later in the century, although it is likely that the arrangement in carels is on the medieval plan. Chains for the books are preserved and it is curious that they were considered necessary at so late a date.

Even with this extension, a long, unused vestibule remained. In modern times this has been furnished with show and book cases, but it is unpanelled on the main wall. The roof over the old library room has been spoiled by ceiling,

H

but over the rest it is intact and is of low pitch, supported at each bay division by massive beams and arched brackets resting on stone corbels. There is a centre purlin only, from which rafters stretch to the wall plates. Lead was originally laid on this roof.

An interesting water course crosses the Camery and the area of the cloisters.[105] It is fed from the springs in the bishop's garden, and enters the Camery at a point where there is now a peep-hole in the wall and an inspection pit close by. The channel is very complicated and of varying section, until it apparently joins an older course near the doorway into the cloister. This uncertain course is probably due to deviations in order to fit in with former buildings on the site.

From the turn by the doorway the stream flows through the dipping place in the garth to the Penniless Porch in the market-place. It then passes under, and used to serve the New Works, twelve houses erected by Beckington's executors about 1460 on the north side of the market-place. At the end of the New Works there is a sharp turn to the south near the present conduit, providing an exit into the mill stream.

The so-called dipping place in the garth was covered over about a century ago to make way for modern graves, and the entrance was destroyed.

Fortunately Carter (1795) had made a detailed drawing. The place was reopened in 1927. It was described by early writers as a gong or privy, but this was later ridiculed when the subsequent course of the stream was discovered under the New Works houses. This, however, cannot be altogether ruled out, as it might have been used for such a purpose all along its course. The New Works were peculiarly situated against the churchyard and had no gardens. We may therefore have an early example of indoor water sanitation. Moreover we know that there was a privy in the area of the cloister garth. On the other hand it must be admitted that the arrangements existing seem to indicate a dipping place in order to give a supply of water to the cathedral. The date of this work is difficult to determine. Buckle says it is Early

English, with a later Perpendicular door (now destroyed).

The inscriptions on the monuments in the cloisters (all post-reformation) were faithfully recorded by Jewers in 1892 and he made use of an older manuscript by Fielder. A considerable number have since been lost by decay, and falling from rusty staples. Recently the Friends of the Cathedral have undertaken some restoration and it is to be hoped that further loss has been prevented. The barbarous treatment of so much beautiful eighteenth century work by those who can only be called the Gothic maniacs of 1845 has been noted elsewhere, and is a warning to all generations to respect the work of their forbears even though it be temporarily out of fashion.

We may consider some of the more important of these pathetic relics beginning with the east cloister walk. Just south of the door into the Camery churchyard we find the fine tablet to the Linley family. It is the only example left in the church of the work of the notable Bath statuary King, and has, of course, recently acquired topical interest. (The marks in the wall south of the north door into the nave, showing its former position, are clearly visible.) Linley, the musician of Bath, was the son of a builder and carpenter once employed on the Badminton estate.[106] Of his beautiful and famous grand-daughters, one, recorded here, was Mrs Sheridan, and the other, Mrs Tickell, lived with her husband for a time in Wells. Mrs Sheridan was brought to the cathedral to be buried after her death at the Hotwells, Clifton. The family must have had some connection with Wells but what it was has never been discovered. Mrs Linley senior may have been a native, although her marriage took place at Bathampton.

Farther south in the cloister is the interesting tablet to Claver Morris, M.D., surmounted by his bust, said to be the only one of this period in Somerset.[107] (This formerly stood against the wall behind the High Altar and facing the Lady Chapel. It closed an old doorway which led into the sanctuary at this point, as the new masonry of 1845 shows.) The bay at the south end of the walk is given up to memorials of the Sherston family and connections, removed from St Catherine's

Chapel. They were engaged as clothiers in the neighbourhood of Bath and came to Wells in the seventeenth century intermarrying with Davis and then with Donnington whose arms they obtained, legally enough, but rather to the indignation of Jewers. They owned much land in the city including the remains of the Priory of St John in Southover on which the Central primary schools were built in 1858.

In the first bay of the south walk was a charming medallion to Lord Francis Seymour, son of a Duke of Somerset, and Dean, who died in 1799. This recently fell and disappeared, but as a measure of reparation the Corporation of Wells has named one of its new roads 'Seymour Close.' Occupying the end of the south walk we find the large and fine monument to Bishop Hooper, removed from the south choir aisle where he lies buried.[108] His arms (doubtful according to Jewers), *Gyronny of eight or and erm., a tower sa.,* are shown impaled with correct arms of the See : *Az, a saltire surmounting a pastoral staff in pale or, betw. on the dexter two keys erect and addorsed, the bows interlaced, one arg., the other of the second, and on the sinister sword erect of the third, hilt and pomel gold.* Hooper was one of the most distinguished post-reformation bishops and was translated from St Asaph, having previously held the deanery of Canterbury. He was a personal friend of Ken who welcomed his translation in 1704 to succeed the quarrelsome Kidder, killed in the great storm of 1703, whom Ken did not recognize as the rightful bishop. From this time, however, he ceased to sign himself as of Bath and Wells.

The west cloister contains the only *Chantrey* monument of the cathedral, that to Mr. Phelips of Montacute, not a very inspiring example, however, of that sculptor's work. Of all those in the choir it probably most deserved removal in 1845 but was suffered to remain owing to family influence. Dean Robinson had it placed here in 1925 on the restoration of St John Baptist's Chapel where it occupied the altar space. Another monument in this walk of some interest is that to John Berkeley Burland, one of the many distinguished grandsons of Dr Claver Morris.[109] The arms on the tablet show those of Morris, 2 and 3. In a large carved medallion is seen a curious deathbed scene.

The outside of the east wall of the cloister, viewed from the Camery churchyard, exhibits much detailed information concerning buildings now destroyed. In 1894, Edmund Buckle, the Diocesan architect, thoroughly excavated the area in front of the wall and thus explained many of the markings,[110] some though, to this day, remain doubtful.

There are very many references in the cathedral documents to the existence of a Lady Chapel (I) at this spot, *juxta claustrum*, from 1243 onwards. We also know that the Saxon bishop Giso (1061–88) endowed *a* Lady Chapel with land at North Wootton.[111] Whether these chapels were one and the same has never been conclusively proved, since only one Saxon stone was found on the site. We have already discussed the possibility that the Saxon cathedral was built here on the banks of the 'Water of Wells,' and, on this theory, an eastern chapel might well be found at this spot, the main cathedral building lying across the cloister garth. On excavation no positive evidence emerged but foundations of a simple rectangular building of the thirteenth century built out at an awkward angle of 75° to the cloister wall were found. This would be the Lady Chapel *juxta claustrum,* and it is a fair inference, but nothing more, that it stood on earlier foundations. Had the original foundations been contemporary with the cloister wall such an awkward angle would hardly have been chosen. The doorway to this thirteenth century chapel may now be clearly seen behind the later Stillington perpendicular masonry.

It is known that the Bitton family more or less took over the thirteenth century chapel for their own tombs, perhaps because another Lady Chapel (II) had become available in the main church. Numerous obits were established for the family, and the excavations showed the addition of an aisle on each side, later in the thirteenth century, probably during the time of Dean Bitton (1284–92). This of course involved the erection of arcades, and the place where the respond on the south side was torn out of the cloister wall is clearly visible. Its base exists just below ground level. The hole was partly filled, as may be seen, with pieces of Blue Lias shafting. The attachment of the aisle roof may also be followed, but the purpose of the small door behind the privy is not known. It was outside the aisle. Buckle puts the date of the cloister wall in which these relics are found as *c*. 1186, but it has to be remembered that the Early English cloister could not have been completed at that time since the nave was unfinished. Perhaps 1230 would be a better date.

The use of this clearly much venerated chapel for ordinations, etc., may be followed in the cathedral documents up to the time of Bishop Stillington (1466–91). He pulled it down, presumably in 1469, since ordinations in it then suddenly cease, only to be resumed in 1492. Stillington erected a magnificent building in its place as his mausoleum, although it was still to be known as the Lady Chapel *juxta claustrum*. This was almost a separate church with nave (50 feet), crossing (22 feet) and choir (34 feet). There was also a vestry on the north side of the choir (15 feet square). The internal height was thought to be about 40 feet. There seem to have been large tower-like buttresses at the western corners (only) of the transepts. The northernmost of these came very near the stairway in the buttress of the main church transept. This has, some 18 feet from the ground, a blocked-up doorway, and it has been suggested that a bridge existed across to the new chapel. It is a little difficult to see why communication was required at this height.

Some considerable portions of the vault of Stillington's chapel were recovered during the excavations, and are now stacked on the bench of the east cloister. These enabled Mr. Buckle to reconstruct the whole, revealing a magnificent late perpendicular fan vault with pendants, which closely resembled that at Sherborne Abbey. The chapel must also have contained some fine tombs, notably those of Stillington himself and of Precentor Overay who, in his will, left his body to be buried in the New Lady Chapel by the cloister *ante ostium introitus in cancellum dicte capelle retro sepulturam bone memorie domini mei Roberti (Stillington) nuper Bathon. et Wellen. episcopi*. The west end of this chapel remains attached to the cloister wall. Most of it consists of a large 'window' which could only be glazed above the level of the cloister parapet, the top course of which forms a sill above the springing of the window arch. In the centre of this wall is a small quatrefoil hagioscope, so that the interior of the chapel could be seen from the library. The two small windows which now light this part of the library are post-reformation insertions.

Stillington's chapel had a short life, since it was given by Bishop Barlow and the Dean and Chapter in 1552 to Sir John Gates to be broken up. Gates, who was implicated in the Northumberland plot, was executed before the contract was completed, but the damage had been done, and the area was used for many years as a quarry for stone to repair the canonical houses. Godwin says that 'divers olde men,' who had seen the chapel built and the bishop buried, lived also to see the bones of the latter turned out of the leaden casket in which they had been placed.

We have already mentioned the scars left on the south transept wall by the removal of the vestry to St Martin's chapel. There was the other small room, opening into the cloister, just north of the Stillington chapel. It measured 10 feet square. Outside, a portion of the screen opening into the cloister may be seen looking like the head of a perpendicular window of c. 1500. The bench has been cut away inside the cloister. There seems to be no explanation as to the use of this room. It had no connection with the chapel, which already had a large vestry.

CHAPTER IX

THE VICARS' CLOSE

IT became the custom of the Prebendaries of Wells, who often lived on their estates at some distance from the cathedral, to supply substitutes or Vicars to perform their singing and other duties in the church. These clerics, many of them in minor orders, lived in what we should now call lodgings about the town. Bishop Ralph of Shrewsbury in 1348 founded a college for them, partly for their own benefit to give them a more dignified residence, and partly to avoid the scandals which arose for their too close association with the towns-folk.[112] He provided the new body with a remarkable set of buildings which closely resembles the colleges at Oxford and Cambridge and which is still virtually intact. But, in-stead of the usual quadrangle, a double row of cells or lodgings, forty-four in all, was built, complete with chapel at one end and dining-hall at the other. There was only one entrance, through a large arch under the dining-hall, so that control over the inhabitants was easy. This entrance was altered in early perpendicular times. Each cell at first con-sisted of two rooms, one on the ground floor and one on the first, with small closets attached to each. There has been much alteration and adaptation as, since the college survived the reformation, accommodation had to be provided for married members. In particular two cells have frequently been run together to make a comfortable house.

One, however, now No. 22, was carefully restored and re-instated by the Oxford antiquarian, J. H. Parker, who lived in the close for some time. If we look at No. 22 we see that the windows and doorway are what we might expect from the mid-fourteenth century date. The former are of two lights, trefoiled with ogee head, finished square so that two tiny tracery elements are formed. On the ground floor they have a plain transom and are without labels. The closet windows are plain chamfered slits and the door has also a single plain chamfer. Character is now given to the houses by the insertion of the chimney as the result of benefactions of Bishop Beckington †1465. Up to roof level the chimney breast is plain except for a square medallion holding a coat of arms on a shield. The chimney then emerges through the roof into a large square box also displaying a coat of arms, although this is smaller than the lower one, and is backed by a conventional panel-like carving. The chimney box is diminished in two steps before it changes into an octagonal column. This was capped by a beautiful castellated head with octagonal roof, sixteen upright slits being provided for the smoke to emerge.

None of these heads survives in the original stonework and many are missing altogether. All the houses had the arched gateways to their gardens of which now only a few remain, although the others have only been destroyed fairly recently. Parker thought that they were contemporary with the original houses, and it is difficult to contest this suggestion, although they have been dated as late as the fifteenth century.

The arms on the various chimneys are those of Beckington and his three executors, *Swan: a fess betw. three swans' wings raised. Sugar: three sugar loaves and in chief a doctor's cap.* (there is, however, considerable variation in these arms), and *Pope: A chev. betw. in chief two roses and in base a talbot pass.*

It has been suggested that the chapel, built across the north end of the Close, was first erected by the founder, and there is a reference of a gift of some vestments in 1401. Structurally, however, it does not appear to be of a date earlier than the time of Bishop Bubwith (1407–24). The four two-arched early Perpendicular windows date from this time, and so must the door, since it bears the arms of Bubwith. The doorway, which is rather clumsily contrived under one of the window arches, was thought to be an insertion replacing an older door at the west end. There seems, however, to be no evidence for this. The wooden shields bear the following arms :

(1) *Two bars and in chief three roundles (Hungerford).*
(2) *A saltire surmounting a pastoral staff, betw. on the*

> dexter two keys addorsed and erect, the bows inter-
> laced, and on the sinister a sword erect (the See of
> Bath and Wells).
>
> (3) *A chev. charged with a mitre (Bishop Stafford).*
>
> (4) *A fess. eng. betw. twelve holly leaves 4, 4, 4, in quad-*
> *rangles (Bishop Bubwith).*

Bubwith in his will, having left provision, *inter alia,* for the erection of the north-west tower of the cathedral and the library, gives the residue to his executors to carry out certain works about which he had instructed them verbally. One of these was undoubtedly the erection of a large almshouse in the city, still bearing his name, and the arms of his successor Stafford. There can be little doubt that another of these works was the erection of this chapel, the door of which, as we have seen, bears the arms of Bubwith and Stafford, and very significantly of Lord Hungerford, whom Bubwith appointed to superintend the work of his executors.

The structure appears quite homogeneous up to the level of the parapet. Although the windows of the chamber over are square-headed, they resemble in all other respects the larger ones in the chapel below. There is no sign of a western door. The upper room is approached by an external newel stair attached to the neighbouring house, and the three buttresses in front are continuous and of mid-fifteenth century date. The embattled parapet and the bell-cote (the chimney is modern) were clearly added in Bishop Beckington's time. The bell-cote now bears his (restored) arms. There are three niches at the parapet level, but no evidence that they ever contained statues. Of much the same date is the fine, almost flat-arched window which occupies the gabled front of the house next the chapel, and which looks down the close. This has, under its four Perpendicular lights, large panels with carvings of arms: (1) Beckington; (2) The College of Vicars (the Saltire alone); (3) the Saltire, pastoral staff, keys and sword (The See); (4) *Quarterly 1 and 4, A chev. betw. three leopards' faces; 2 and 3, On a fess betw. three leopards' faces as many fleur-de-lys.* This last coat is assigned as to 1 and 4 to Bishop Stillington (1466–91). The second and third quarters are those of members of his family.

The house may have been embellished for the use of the chaplain or some other official of the college. Before leaving this end of the close we should notice the insets of Early English foliage carving in the south face of the chapel wall, between the windows, and in the parapet. It is not known when these were put up or whence they came. Inside, the chapel possesses the only original stone altar mensa in the buildings of the cathedral. It had been sunk level with the floor and has been recently restored. On each side is a row of Perpendicular panels with a large empty niche over. A tiny piscina is contrived in one of the panels on the south. The wooden screen is medieval. In the west wall is a small square aumbry possessing a chimney similar to the one to the south of the Lady Chapel. It may also have contained a constantly burning light.

The most interesting part of the college is the block of buildings which closes the southern end and forms the entrance to it. This allows vehicles to pass, while there is also a wicket gate at the side. To the west were small storerooms. Then, following the usual medieval plan of having the principal rooms on the first floor was made the fine dining-hall over, approached by a newel staircase. A small kitchen is provided also at first floor level over store rooms. There are good windows high up in the east and west walls containing orthodox Decorated tracery, each of three lights.

Originally the room was also lit by four windows on the north side and three on the south. Several of these remain and consist of two cinquefoiled lights with ogee moulding leading to a large central tracery light. They have transoms and seem perhaps rather advanced in design for the mid-century, so possibly the dining-hall was not built for a few years after the living accommodation was provided. This room has a plain barrel roof of contemporary date, which was probably always plastered and, mercifully, has not been stripped.

The two interesting wooden statues over the High Table at the east end also belong to this period. They represent the Annunciation. Beneath the figure of Our Lady kneel the Three Kings in adoration, while at the feet of the angel, two boys, our Lord and St John Baptist, are playing. The hall must have remained in use in this form until the time of Bishop Beckington or his executors a century or more later.

This bishop had almost a mania for building imposing gateways, and five may be attributed to him in Wells. From this dining-hall to the cathedral he spanned the gap by what has long been known, perhaps because of its method of closure, as the Chain Gate. At the same time, and we cannot know which purpose was paramount, a covered way was provided from college to the great church. This Gate is beautifully designed and, because of its double function, unique in England. It is made essentially as a gateway, and then continued as a bridge to the cathedral. From the west we can see a large four-centred arch spanning the carriage-way which, incidentally, for several centuries carried all the traffic to London and the east. The arch rises to a pronounced string course running right from the college to the chapter house stairs. This is really a double course, the hollowed band containing strips of carving at regular intervals. All this carving has perished on the more exposed west side, but on the east some beautiful pieces remain. These consist of recumbent angels with fillet and cross, and groups made up of the stags' heads and pheons of the Beckington arms.

In the tympanum of the main arch are carved various parts of the rebus of Beckington, the beacon, tun, etc. On the east side, however, the carvings are just conventional cusped circles. Two smaller arches, again four-centred, provide for the footways. They only rise to half the height of the road arch, and the blank spaces above are covered with plain Perpendicular panelling arranged in two triplets. Shafts which frame this panelling and the arches, rise from the ground to circular capitals which are part of the first string course. These capitals support small, square, diagonally placed, panelled buttresses, which are now carried upwards to frame the set of four windows. They end in pinnacles carried above the roof, a prominent feature of the façade. Since five buttresses are required to frame the four windows, an extra central one springs from a large corbel over the middle arch. This seems to have been supported by an angel with outstretched wings. The two wide windows over the roadway have very flat four-centred arches. They are of three lights but the centre one forms a niche for statues. The northern figure on the western side was St Andrew, as portions of the saltire are visible. That on the south may have been an ecclesiastic, since there are indications of fringed ends of a stole. The two figures on the east are quite unrecognizable. One is bearded and they are in flowing surplice-like garments. A common dripstone to the windows runs right across the bridge, even being carried round the buttresses. The two windows over the pavements are of two lights only, and so without statues. All the windows have a plain transom and closely resemble, as may have been intended, those of the previous century which light the dining-hall. South of the main gateway section, the bridge is supported for a distance by a plain ashlar wall until a substantial buttress is reached. This serves to frame a large plain arch which carries the passage right against the old end window of the chapter house staircase. The dripstone of this window is still visible on the outside. Within, of course, the window has had the glass removed, and the actual footway is carried through a Tudor-like four centred-arch. The stairs descend from the bridge through this window cum doorway, although this is masked from the outside.

The southern portion of the bridge is lit by three-light windows, replicas of those over the roadway, although without statues or transoms. The wall between them is left plain, and rather unsatisfactory buttresses spring from corbels at parapet level, serving to match those over the roadway. The parapet is of wide cinquefoiled blank panels rising to the top of castellations with small linking rectangles between. It is most effective. There formerly existed, attached to the plain wall on the south, a curious building erected in the seventeenth century to house sessions records. It was taken away about 1867.

The eastern side of the bridge is not so impressive, as the façade is broken, and the construction complex. South of the road the plain ashlar masonry is replaced by random coursing of local stone, and a square window lights the hollow interior. The passageway over the roadway is partitioned off by a constructional wall and doorway on the south, but is then continued one bay farther to form a landing open to the stairs which lead downwards to the cathedral from this point. All this complication is masked on the west side, but on the east we can see that the bridge façade only stretches for the one bay of the landing, when it is abruptly returned to the west to meet the much narrower staircase. The main irregularity, however, is due to the fact that the bridge, crossing the road at right-angles from the chapter house stairs, hits the vicars' dining-hall too far to the west.

To obtain entry to the right part of the hall a passage has been built out running eastwards over the pavement. This forms a large lobby with a window facing east. Under the window is a square panel containing two angels holding the Beckington arms, which is now hopelessly decayed. On the southern face of the lobby, also under a window, is a finely preserved panel of the arms alone. The passageway over the road and pavements is wide and may have been used also for other purposes.

On the landing there has recently been collected a number of interesting carved stones. Their origin is quite unknown. They were formerly lying loose at the side of the stairs and on the bench of the north choir aisle. Apart from one or two heads of the fourteenth they seem to have been carved in the early years of the thirteenth century about the time when the west front was building. They have not, however, been removed from the front as there is no place where they would fit. Other carving of the same date is found on the front of the Chapel of the Close and at Mellifont 'Abbey,' an eighteenth century building at Wookey. One suggestion is that it came from the older cloister of Bishop Jocelin, if indeed that was of stone. There is here a good representation of the fable of the Fox and Goose, and a church-like building either in a boat, in which case it may represent the ark, or surrounded by walls.

The exact date of the staircase wing which was added to the dining-hall on the north side, within the college precinct, is unknown. It nowhere contains any indication of a particular donor. Had Beckington or his executors been responsible we should almost certainly have found a rebus or arms upon it. It is a reasonable assumption that it was built by the College itself in the fifteenth century. A fine wide stone staircase runs straight up to the hall which it meets exactly opposite the corresponding exit to the cathedral on the south. Above the stairs, rooms on two levels are contrived. Thus at the northern end there is a lobby at ground level, a 'secret' treasury above, and main treasury above that. As the stairs rise, they replace the space of the first floor, which contains only the northern room. By the main door into the hall is a curious alcove apparently for a doorkeeper. Just by the door on the east we find a newel stair leading to the rooms. It rises into a chamber on the second floor which has recently been called the 'Exchequer.' Whether such a name indicates its use in medieval times is doubtful, since it is remarkably well furnished for a mere office. The head of the stairs is protected in the usual Tudor manner with a wooden surround, and there is a large contemporary fireplace and lavabo. We find a similar lavabo in the ante-room of the dining-hall of the deanery, so it seems not unlikely that this was also an ante-room where the vicars assembled before dining. Its position, however, is not very convenient for this purpose. No doubt when dining in common ceased and vicars lived with their families in the Close, the room came to be used as an 'exchequer' for the storage of deeds, etc., concerned with the considerable estates of the college. Indeed a box for such documents remains therein.

Leading out of this room we come to a smaller compartment which was probably the medieval exchequer. Inside is a most interesting chest of small drawers marked on their fronts with differing designs of brass nails. From this inner chamber a newel stair descends to another below it, forming the first floor of the whole block. No doubt this inner 'inner' room would make a secure treasury, and its very existence might not be suspected. It was called the 'secret treasury' from the fact that there is a trap door, obviously of medieval date, in the floor of the upper room leading down into it.

It would not be secret, however, to any one entering the upper room, as the newel stair is obvious enough, and forms a much more convenient means of entry. Possibly it is a later addition.

In the next century some further improvements were made to the hall by Richard Pomeroy.[113] As the glass shows, he built the two fine oriel windows, north and south, to light the high table, replacing those of the fourteenth century. A much plainer oriel at the far end of the room, looking up the close, must also be attributed to Pomeroy. It contains two small rondels of stained glass, one of the symbols of the Passion, and the other with the letters POM. A stone shield near the southern oriel has the saltire of the vicars and lettering arranged so : RICUS at the top, PO and ME in the side arms, and ROY at the bottom.

The plain but pleasant fireplace is of the same date as the chimneys of the close, since it bears the initials of Sugar, executor to Beckington. Over it, forming a mantelshelf, is an addition of the time of Pomeroy having five shields with this writing between them : *In vets pcibs he'at Co me do'm Ricardu Pomroy quem salvet' Jh's Amen,* i.e. *In vestris precibus habeatis commendatum Dominum Ricardum Pomerum quem salvet Jesus Amen.* The five shields are painted on the stone and date from the time of Bishop Clerk, 1523–41.

(1) *Or, two bars az., surmounted by a horse's head erased erm. and in chief three escallop shells gu., Clerk.*

(2) Beckington.

(3) The Tudor Royal Arms.

(4) The See.

(5) Pomeroy.

There is nothing to indicate a date for the little reading pulpit contrived over the fireplace, since the window lighting it is quite new. The remaining linen-fold panelling of the hall is presumably sixteenth century of the time of Pomeroy. Some of the benches and other furniture may be much older. A beautiful late Georgian gallery has just been removed from the west end. It replaced an earlier one on which an organ stood and which may have gone back to the time of Dr

Claver Morris, *c.* 1715. For some long time the Hall was available for public meetings and particularly concerts, being known as 'Close Hall.'[114]

The painting over the mantelpiece is of particular interest and shows the granting of the original charter by Bishop Ralph in 1348. It was, however, painted at the time of the renewed charter of Elizabeth, granted in 1592. It shows the Priest and Lay Vicars in their habits of that date. Godwin says it was a copy of an older wall painting at the foot of the hall stairs, and this seems likely enough.[115]

NOTES

ABBREVIATIONS

Calendar of MSS. of the Dean and Chapter of Wells, Vol. I
(1907); II (1914). Her Majesty's Stationery Office   CM
Proceedings of the Somerset Archaeological Society   SAS
Somerset Record Society   SRS
Early History of the Church of Wells. Canon C. M. Church.
Barnicoat & Pearce, 1894   Church
Lives of the Bishops of Bath and Wells. S. H. Cassan.
Rivington, 1829   Cassan
Wells Cathedral, Its Inscriptions and Heraldry. A. J. Jewers.
Mitchell & Hughes, 1892   Jewers
*Wells Cathedral. Its Foundation, Constitutional History and
Statutes.* H. E. Reynolds. 1881   Reynolds
Notes and Queries for Somerset and Dorset   NQSD

[1] The primary source of information about the early church at Wells
is contained in the documents of the Chapter Library. There are three
great books of miscellaneous documents, *Liber Albus I,* sometimes
called R₁; *Liber Albus II,* or R₃; and *Liber Ruber,* or R₂; together
with many charters and similar material. These have received much
attention from the Historical Manuscripts Commission, and the following books have been published by it: *Report on the MSS. of
Wells Cathedral.* J. A. Bennet, 1885. H.M.S.O.; *Calendars of MSS.
of the Dean and Chapter of Wells,* I (1907); II (1914). H.M.S.O.
Early historians of the cathedral church based their work almost
entirely on these documents. Francis Godwin, Bishop of Llandaff and
of Hereford, and son of a bishop of Bath and Wells of 1584-90, published an account in his *De Praesulibus Anglie Commentarius* (1615).
Wharton in his *Anglia Sacra* (I, 553ff.) prints two narratives com-
bined in one, taken from *Liber Albus II* (297-302), sometimes called
'the Canon of Wells.' These have now been disentangled and made
available as *Historia Major* and *Historia Minor* in Vol. 39, pp. 48ff.,
of the Somerset Record Society. In a portion of a Bath Chartulary,
and therefore quite an independent document, now preserved at
Lincoln's Inn, Joseph Hunter found a narrative of Wells history on
which Wharton's two accounts were obviously based. He called this
Historiola, and published it with most valuable notes in the Camden
Society's Ecclesiastical Documents No. I, 1840. Later writers have
made much use of the *Historia Major* and *Historia Minor.* Thus
Edmund Archer (†1739), Archdeacon of Taunton, produced his
Chronicon Wellense, sive Annales Ecclesiae Cathedralis Wellensis.
H. E. Reynolds, in an enormous privately printed volume of 1881
breaks new ground in that he gives in addition the *Ordinale et Statuta
Ecclesiae Cathedralis Wellensis,* a Lambeth Library document No. 729.
He also prints excerpts from a MS. history by Nathaniel Chyle who
was secretary to Bishop Mews (1673-84). Another MS. recently printed
and edited by Dom Aelred Watkin is the so-called *Dean Cosyn's MS.*
This is mostly concerned with ritual directions and legal controversy

which the dean extracted from earlier documents. He was at Wells 1499-1525, and was a nephew of Bishop Oliver King. It is printed in *Somerset Record Society*, Vol. 56.

[2] J. A. Robinson, *The Saxon Bishops of Wells*. British Academy, O.U.P., undated, p. 5

[3] 'De Antiquitate Ecclesiae Glastoniensis' in Hearne's *Adam of Domerham*. Oxford, 1727. For discussion of this source see J. A. R. Robinson, *Somerset Historical Essays*. British Academy, London, 1921, p. 2.

[4] *De Praesulibus Anglie,* p. 363. Ed. of 1743.

[5] Dugdale's *Monasticon,* Vol. II, No. II, p. 286. Ed. of 1819.

[6] SRS, Vol. 39, p. 49.

[7] *The Saxon Bishops of Wells.* See note 2.

[8] Later the remaining stump of Sherborne was to unite with Ramsbury at some date between 1041 and 1058. The united diocese was described as "Wiltunensis,' but whether the throne was at Ramsbury, Sherborne, or Wilton near Salisbury, is not known. Perhaps all three places were used by the bishop, Herman. The see was removed to Old Sarum in the eighth decade of the century, and there followed of course the further migration to Salisbury (New Sarum) in the thirteenth century.

[9] *The Saxon Bishops of Wells,* p. 44, n. 2.

[10] J. A. Robinson, 'Effigies of Saxon Bishops at Wells' in *Archaeologia*, LXV, p. 95. This paper by Dean Robinson is excellent for details of the exhumation and for photographs. The actual effigies are described, however, in greater detail by Dr Fryer in SAS, LXI, p. 26.

[11] SAS, LX, 118.

[12] SAS, XL, 32.

[13] SAS, XI, 20.

[14] The somewhat complicated story of the three Lady Chapels at Wells has been expanded by the writer in NQSD, XXVI, pp. 126, 168.

[15] R₁ f. 31 and f. 41 (see note 1); also SAS, XL, 21.

[16] G. F. Brown, SAS, XL, 275 and XXXVI, 70.

[17] SAS, LV, 84.

[18] H. E. Balch, *The Water Courses of Wells.* Wells Archaelogical Society Proceedings, 1925.

[19] Church, p. 25.

[20] *Historiola* (see note 1), p. 25.

[21] *Archaeologia*, LXV, p. 94.

[22] It was said that he was born before his father's consecration, although trouble was later caused by the relationship. It was not unusual in those days for laymen to be appointed bishops and to receive the lesser orders in a few days.

[23] J. Collinson, *History of Somerset,* III, 398.

[24] Church.

[25] *Archaeological Journal,* Vol. 85, pp. 2, 29.

[26] ibid.

[27] NQSD, XXVI, 126.

[28] This tomb was formerly thought to be that of Canon Storthwaite, executor of Bubwith, but the present attribution has been conclusively proved by A. S. Bicknell (one of the family) in SAS, XL, 179. It is also indicated by Leland. *In superiori transepto versus*

meridiem jacet in elegantibus tumulis, 2 episcopi et quidam Bikenelle, Canonicus Wellensis. SAS, XXIII, 108.

[29] A rubbing of this inscription is given by A. B. Connor, SAS, LXXXII, 183.

[30] The tomb was attributed in the nineteenth century by Jewers and others to Dean Husee, 1302-5, probably because his obit was celebrated at St Calixtus's altar. This, however, is an impossibly early date. Sir W. St John Hope then suggested Thomas Boleyn, Precentor of Wells, and a relative of the famous Anne (†1470). He did this because the arms of Bullen of Stickford, Co. Lincoln were given by Burke as: *Silver Fretty and a chief sable with three silver rondels on the chief.* At present all that is certain is the black colour of the fretty. Hope also says that there is a carving at the east end, of clerks singing from a prayer desk, indicating presumably a precentor. If this ever existed it has disappeared. Dean Robinson accepts the attribution, and has a long article on Boleyn in SAS, LXI, I, but A. C. Fryer, SAS, LXIX, 21 considers that the tomb cannot be later than 1450. Recently L. S. Colchester has pointed out that the arms so far as they can now be deciphered, are those of Rogers. They appear in the south choir window of St John's Church, Glastonbury: *Argent, fretty sable, a chief gules.* No such name, however, can be discovered in connection with the cathedral at this time.

[31] *Archaeological Journal,* LXI, 155 and Church, for detailed drawings of the tomb by Roland Paul, p. 289; A. C. Fryer, SAS, LXVI, 51.

[32] CM, I, 213: . . . *pro quo altissimus incessanter virtuosa miracula indies operari non desistit, celebria miracula que potencia fiunt ad laudem recolendi viri Willelmi de Marchia . . .*

[33] Sir William St John Hope suggested during a visit by the Archaeological Institute to Wells in 1904 that this tomb was in fact the canopy to an altar attached to the Marcia tomb, and moved round from an eastern to a southern position in post-reformation times. This suggestion, however, cannot now be accepted. The lighting arrangements show the canopy to be *in situ.* There is no sign of an altar or piscina, nor was a chantry ever established for this bishop. It would have been necessary to take the canopy right down and rebuild in its present position between say 1540 and 1790, when it is recorded in this position in Gough's *Sepulcralia.* It is dfficult to believe that this trouble would have been taken during a period when scant respect was paid to similar monuments, many of which were wantonly destroyed or fell into ruin. The base of the tomb is of Purbeck Marble and so is later than that of Bishop Marcia which is of Blue Lias.

[34] In an endeavour to establish the actual burial place of Lady Lisle a large ledger stone at the entrance to the north transept was raised by Canon Church, *Archaeological Journal,* LXI, 7. The stone has the matrix of a brass, outlining what appears to be a female figure of the fifteenth century. No evidence was found beyond a lock of fair hair. Incidentally the resting places of all the bishops are known so that this mysterious tomb cannot belong to one of them.

[35] J. A. Robinson, NQSD, XIII, 347.

[36] St Sidwell is represented in several stained glass windows in Somerset, and a church was dedicated to her at Exeter. She is, however, usually shown carrying her own head and holding a scythe,

the instrument of her martyrdom A similar story is told of St Urith. For full details see C. Woodforde, *Stained Glass in Somerset*, p. 188, n. 5.

[37] Jewers, 146. Mrs J. A. Robinson has edited a diary of Bishop Kidder, SRS, Vol. 37.

[38] Bishop Valens, a suffragan to Bishop Beckington, had been appointed by the Pope as 'of Tenos.' This was in 1459, and it seemed to require four documents: (1) Valens, provided to the bishopric of Tenos, directed to repair thither and not to perform any episcopal functions outside his diocese; (2) Restrictions removed; (3) Allowed to retain the rectory of Lydeard St Lawrence, there being no income from the 'diocese'; (4) Granted 100 gold florins per annum out of the income of the bishopric of Bath and Wells.

[39] 'The Wells Clock,' R. P. Howgrave-Graham. Friends of Wells Cathedral, 1973.

[40] This lettering is pre-reformation, probably original, painted over 1727.

[41] It is thought that the Arabic numerals were repainted in the seventeenth century.

[42] This seems best translated as 'This sphere represents the world in miniature, its original.' On a tile of the pavement near the High Altar of Westminster Abbey (*c.* 1270), the same sentence appears except that *microcosmum* is more correctly rendered as *macrocosmum*.

[43] SAS, XCVI, 230; *Archaeological Journal*, LXXXV, 16.

[44] Church, 76-7; SAS, XCVI, 230.

[48] Personal testimony of the grandson of the man employed.

[49] See plan, Church, p. 1.

[50] CM, 2, p. 232. It is decreed that the obit of Bishop Bubwith shall cease in ten years, i.e. on January 8th, 1522-3. But a chaplain was appointed again in 1537 and in 1543 Further information about these nave altars may be obtained from the index to CM, Vol. 2.

[51] CM, 2, 115.

[52] C. Woodforde, *Stained Glass in Somerset*. O.U.P., 1946, p. 212.

[53] A. B. Connor, SAS, LXXXII, 196 and NQSD. XVIII, 214-15.

[54] Francis Bond, *Gothic Architecture in England*, p. 172.

[55] *Liber Albus,* f. 4, 120, 128. We read of two tapers to burn in St Mary's Chapel, behind the High Altar, and *Item lego imagini beatae Mariae in capella retro magnum altare in ecclesia beatae Andreae Wellensi, unum keverchef de serio, pretio quinque solidos.*

[56] Church, p. 1. Apart from this somewhat unjustified speculation, this is an excellent plan, and it is a pity that more attention has not been paid to it by subsequent writers and those responsible for labelling chapels and tombs.

[57] Our Lord is seated in Benediction in the centre, with St Peter on his right hand and St Andrew on his left. These are the gift of Mrs. Head, donor of the Rood. They are the work of A. G. Walker. On the south side are SS David and George, given by the Somerset Freemasons. On the north are SS Patrick and Dunstan given by Mrs Head.

[58] Register of Drokensford, f. 242, quoted by Church, p. 308.

[59] J. Britton, *History and Antiquities of Wells Cathedral*, 1823, p. 103.

[60] In 1640 the Dean and Chapter order the stairs to the galleries

to be closed (CM, II, 422), 'because it is a thing uncomely and unusuall in cathedrall churches to have galleries sett up.' Some repair to the galleries was ordered, however, in 1701 (CM, II, 482). In 1740 two new galleries were ordered to be set up on the north and south sides next the organ loft for the use of the canons' families. These would seem to have been facing east over the stalls of the Dean and Precentor. It may well be that the earlier gallery only existed on the north and south sides of the choir.

⁶¹ A. C. Fryer, SAS, LXIX, 26; NQSD, VI, 292; A. F. Judd, *The Life of Thomas Bekynton*. Regnum Press 1961.

⁶² A. C. Fryer's description of these tombs is invaluable. For his general discussion on the use of alabaster see SAS, LXVI, 37. For an account of the port and borough of Reckley see NQSD, VI, 151, 362 and VII, 139 with IX, 330.

⁶³ For a fuller discussion of this problem see R. D. Reid in NQSD, XXVI, 121 and NQSD, XIV, 270.

⁶⁴ SRS, XVI, 361.

⁶⁵ For a recent account of his life see C. Woodforde in *Stained Glass in Somerset*, p. 132.

⁶⁶ SRS, XVI, 361. This image of our Lady in Childbed, i.e. the Nativity, was no doubt that referred to in an inspeximus of 1384, C. MSS. I, 381, 'at the altar of St Katherine by the Jesima.' Gunthorpe himself gave a massive silver-gilt image of our Lady to the cathedral in 1487. It weighed 163 ounces, C. MSS. II, 106.

⁶⁷ Henry Hawley was the son of William who purchased the Priory of the Order of St John of Jerusalem at Buckland (Durston, Som.). This interesting House, unique in England, consisted of a large Priory for women, now almost entirely destroyed, and a separate smaller establishment called the Preceptory, for men. It is not certain whether the fine house adjoining the parish church of Durston was the actual Preceptory or a Manor belonging to the establishment. It was occupied by the Hawley family even after they had obtained a peerage. J. Hugo, SAS, X, 1; A. B. Connor, SAS, LXXXII, 184 and Ogilvy's Map, c. 1650.

⁶⁸ A translation by Lord Justice Coleridge is:

> My worse part lives, my better buried lies,
> Death is my life, that he may live he dies,
> To earth I trust these ashes and my woe,
> Till to this dust I too as dust may go.

> Tis thus disconsolate a widow sings,
> T.P., her cousin, hopes for better things.

See also *All's Well that Ends Well* by E. M. Church, Wells, c. 1910, for some account of the family and speculation about the curious epitaph.

⁶⁹ St Stephen (Pope) appears in the glass of the north window. There has been much confusion about the dedications of these two chapels on the north of the retro-choir. In the C. MSS. I and II there are five references to the altar (singular) of St John and St Stephen. There are in addition six records of the altar of St John. It is very likely that the latter refer to St John Baptist, and at least it seems clear that the dedications to St Stephen and St John Evangelist were in one chapel. As late as in a Communar's account

for 1557-8 there is reference to charges at 'St John's and St Stephen's aulter.' There seems no evidence at all for assigning the altar in the choir transept adjoining to St John Evangelist. The error probably arose from these many references to both saints in one breath, as it were, the assumption being made that St John had a separate altar next to that of St Stephen. Dedications to the evangelists were rare in the fourteenth century. Later there may have been some protestant reluctance to give the right title to the Corpus Christi altar and chapel.

[70] J. A. Robinson, SAS, LXXI, 78, where also both poems of Huish are quoted in full.

[71] *Archaeological Journal*, Vol. 88, p. 159. Formidable arguments are here marshalled in favour of a date not later than 1305. The suggestion is made that the building was at least started by Dean Thomas Button before his election as Bishop of Exeter in 1292. There is no doubt that his relative, Bishop Button I, is buried here before the altar, but as he died in 1264 his body must have been moved either from the Lady Chapel I *juxta claustrum,* which was virtually a Button chantry, or from Lady Chapel II.

[72] Register of Drokensford, f. 252b.

[73] Bowen, Serel MSS. Somerset Record Office, quoted by Church, p. 420.

[74] Church, p. 318.

[75] The reference to this entry is Arundel MS.. 2, f. 27, being a letter book of Abbot Monynton. Further entries of interest to Wells are f. 14v, April 20th, 1354, in which stone is granted *pro reparacione manse choristarum,* and another of April 7th, 1365, *pro fabrica ecclesie cathedralis Well'*, f. 79v.

[76] R. i, f. 50d and Church, p. 230.

[77] R. i, f. 51 ; Charter 41a.

[78] Hugh afterwards became Bishop of Lincoln, but retained an affection for his native place leaving money for the fabric in his will. He must not be confused with the almost contemporary St Hugh of Lincoln, who also had connections with Somerset, being at one time Prior of Witham.

[79] For a full account of these masons see John Harvey *English Mediaeval Architects,* Batsford, 1954. The documents at Wells throw no light on the extent to which the master masons *(lathami)* were responsible for design, as opposed to supervision. Lock had a house in the Liberty and £1 6s. 8d. retaining fee. The maximum yearly wage of a craftsman at this time was £7 10s. The house of the master mason was in Byestewalls, now St Andrew Street, and is supposed to be that next the Vicars' Close on the east. This has a tower which may have assisted the mason in his supervisory duties.

[80] J. A. Robinson, SAS, 60, ii, 55. The stone of the front is of the very finest 'Doulting' quality. Nowhere does it exhibit the porous character found elsewhere in the building. This latter, which is easily recognized, has been designated 'Chilcote stone,' from the fact that it is found at that hamlet two miles east of Wells. It is very obvious in the south transept of the cathedral, and it has been suggested that Reginald's church was built of stone from Chilcote because of the distance of Doulting. Such a theory will not, however, bear investigation (valuable though it might have been for dating

purposes) as the porous stone is found in other parts of the cathedral and ancillary buildings. It is found also in many Mendip churches and for such rough purposes as gate posts.

[81] B. Ferrey discovered that the groups of Resurrection statuary were numbered, and that the numerals to the north were Arabic, and on the south Roman. This shows an early use of arabic numerals in England, since they only came to Europe about 1202. They were known to Roger Bacon. It is possible that their use here was at the time the towers were built when blocks of statuary may have been taken down and replaced. SAS, 34, 62.

[82] *Historia Major,* SRS, 39, p. 69. *Iste ad constructionem occidentalis turris in parte australi Wellensis ecclesie duas partes expensarum apposuit.*

[83] L. S. Colchester in *Report of Friends of Wells Cathedral,* 1953. Cal. MSS., ii, 87.

[84] Somerset is the county *par excellence* of Perpendicular towers and, naturally enough, many of these are based upon cathedral models. Much has been written about them, especially by Dr F. J. Allen, SAS, 50, ii, p. 1; 51, ii, p. 1; 58, ii, p. 1; and *The Great Church Towers of England,* C.U.P., 1932. Elaborate geographical systems of classification have been devised by Dr Allen and others (A. K. Wickham, *The Churches of Somerset,* Phoenix House, 1952), but the work in the individual parishes was probably much more independent than such writers would have us believe. There are, of course, broad divisions by date, and these long blank panels belong in Somerset to early Perpendicular days, and would be used at that time in whatever geographical region the church happened to be situated. It is notable that at least two important towers can be dated by documents as after the breach with Rome, since Chewton Mendip and Batcombe were both built in 1541. A special connection between Wells and Yeovil has been suggested, with the probability that the same 'architect,' Wynford, was responsible. Certainly the dates correspond, since the vicar, Robert de Samborne, died in 1382 leaving the residue of his estate to the building of Yeovil church. Moreover, Samborne was a canon of Wells. We look in vain, however, for much similarity in the towers save for such detail as window tracery and parapets, which inevitably mark the period.

[85] Bubwith's will is in the Archiepiscopal Register at Lambeth: Chicheley, 1414, I, f. 378 D. A full translation is given in *Architectural Antiquities of the City of Wells.* J. H. Parker, 1866.

[86] J. H. Parker, *Architecture of the City of Wells,* 1866, p. 44.

[87] SAS, XL, 42.

[88] CM, II, 86.

[89] Jewers, p. 161.

[90] SAS, XXXIII, 60.

[91] CM, II, 206.

[92] Bryan Little, *The Monmouth Episode,* 1956, p. 221.

[93] CM, II, 351.

[94] CM, II, 129 and 171.

[95] MS. 210, Corpus Christi College, Cambridge. Wm Wor: 'Itinerary,' ed. Harvey, Oxford 1969, 289.

[96] CM, II, 214.

[97] CM, II, 538.

[98] CM, I, 273.

[99] CM, I, 381.

[100] CM, I, 384.

[101] R. V. Sellers, *Proceedings Wells Archaeological Society*, 1961.

[102] SRS, 50, p. 528.

[103] ibid., 52, p. 84.

[104] CM, I, p. 520.

[105] SAS, XL, 32 and Church, 425.

[106] Clementina Black, *The Linleys of Bath*, 1926.

[107] *A West Country Physician*, Edited by E. Hobhouse, Simpkin Marshall, 1933. He has left in this diary a unique record of the life of a country doctor in a cathedral city in the early eighteenth century. The fine house which he built himself in 1699 is still intact and faces down the North Liberty.

[108] 'Saml. Tufnell West' Fecit.'

[109] 'J. Bacon Jun', Sculptor, London.'

[110] E. Buckle, in SAS, XL, 33.

[111] Church, p. 19.

[112] CM, I, 162, and many other references of this kind.

[113] Richard Pomeroy was sworn Master of the Fabric in 1488. Reynolds, p. 173.

[114] E. Hobhouse, *Diary of a West Country Physician*. Simpkin Marshall, 1933.

[115] The Vicars are saying:

> *Per vicos positi, pater alme, rogamus.*
> *Ut simul uniti, te dante domus maneamus.*

and the Bishop replies:

> *Vestra petunt merita quod sint concessa petita.*
> *Ut maneatis ita, loca fecimus hic stabilita.*

> Dispersed about the town we humbly pray
> Together through thy bounty dwell we may.

> For your demands deserts do plead I will do what you crave
> To this purpose established, here dwellings you shall have.

A long Latin elegiac verse with references to Queen Elizabeth is on the picture. It is only possible to read a few words of this (1961), and the painting is in poor condition. In a photograph published by Prebendary Parnell in 1926 it is possible to decipher most of it, and Mr. Parnell gives a translation. Phelps, *History of Somersetshire*, II, p. 72, gives the Latin text. For general information about the College of Vicars see the two booklets, *The Chapel of the Vicars' Close, Wells* and *The College of Vicars' Choral, Wells* by H. Parnell. Pettigrew, Wells, *c.* 1925. *The Architectural Antiquities of The City of Wells*, J. H. Parker, 1866, contains some excellent line drawings, but very little information about the college. See aso R. D. Reid, 'Mediaeval Town Planning. The College of Vicars at Wells' in *Country Life*, December 4th, 1958.

THE BISHOPS

909 Athelm	997 Alfwy
923 Wulfhelm I	999 Lyfing
926 Ælfheah	1013 Æthelwine
938 Wulfhelm II	1024 Brihtwig
956 Brihthelm	1033 Dudoc
974 Cyneward	1060 Giso
975 Sigar	

BISHOPS OF BATH

1088 John de Villula	1136 Robert of Lewes
1123 Godfrey	1174 Reginald Fitzjocelyn

BISHOP OF BATH AND GLASTONBURY

1192 Savaric

BISHOP OF BATH

1206 Jocelyn of Wells

BISHOPS OF BATH AND WELLS

1244 Roger	1584 Thomas Godwin
1247 William Bytton I	1593 John Still
1265 Walter Giffard	1608 James Montague
1266 William Bytton II	1616 Arthur Lake
1275 Robert Burnell	1626 William Laud
1293 William March	1628 Leonard Mawe
1302 Walter Haselshaw	1629 Walter Curl
1309 John Drokensford	1632 William Piers
1329 Ralph of Shrewsbury	1670 Robert Creyghton
1363 John Barnet	1673 Peter Mews
1367 John Harewell	1685 Thomas Ken
1386 Walter Skirlaw	1691 Richard Kidder
1388 Ralph Erghum	1704 George Hooper
1401 Henry Bowet	1727 John Wynne
1407 Nicholas Bubwith	1743 Edward Willes
1425 John Stafford	1774 Charles Moss
1443 Thomas Beckington	1802 Richard Beadon
1466 Robert Stillington	1824 G. H. Law
1492 Richard Fox	1845 Richard Bagot
1495 Oliver King	1854 R. J. Eden, Baron Auckland
1504 Hadrian de Castello (Cardinal)	1869 Lord A. C. Hervey
	1894 G. W. Kennion
1518 Thomas Wolsey (Cardinal)	1921 St John B. W. Willson
1523 John Clerk	1937 Francis Underhill
1541 William Knight	1943 J. W. C. Wand
1548 William Barlow (Deprived)	1946 H. W. Bradfield
1554 Gilbert Bourne (Deprived)	1960 E. B. Henderson
1560 Gilbert Berkeley	

GLOSSARY

ABACUS. The top of a capital.

ALB. A white vestment, girdled, usually worn under the chasuble.

ALMUCE. A vestment of a medieval canon. Something like a hood, made of fur with two strips hanging down in front, often laced together.

AMICE. A scarf worn round the neck to protect other vestments.

ARCADE. A row of piers usually dividing nave and choir from aisles.

ASHLAR. Masonry with an even face built of squared blocks.

BOSS. A bunch of ornamental carving, usually at the junction of vaulting ribs.

CAPITAL. The top ornamental portion of a pier or shaft, from neck to abacus.

CASTELLATION. The top of a piece of building resembling a castle.

CELL (of VAULT). A definite division of the vault, usually between shafting corbels, and repeated as required.

CHAMFER. The result of cutting back a sharp edge of masonry, usually the jamb of a window or door.

CORBEL. A fairly heavy stone projecting from a wall to hold an ornament or often the bunch of ribs of a vault.

CROCKET. A decoration, usually a bunch of foliage, placed along the sloping sides of spires, pinnacles, etc.

CUSP. Small pointed projections in the tracery of a window.

DALMATIC. The principal vestment of the deacon. When bishops are fully, i.e. pontifically, vested they wear this vestment under the chasuble, indicating that they have also received orders as deacon.

DOG TOOTH. Typical Early English ornament and found early in that period. A row of four pointed stars. Frequently confused with Norman and Transitional Chevron moulding which has a zig-zag outline.

FERETORY. A place, nearly always behind the High Altar, reserved for the shrine of an important saint, perhaps the patron of the church.

FILLET. A ridge along an Early English roll. It has a square face unlike a keel which is sharp and earlier.

FINIAL. The finishing ornament to a gable or pinnacle, etc. Sometimes they are very large, when they have been vulgarly likened to a cabbage.

HATCHING. The surface of early masonry (ashlar) was produced by the use of an axe, and the ridges run crossways, not horizontal or vertical. Later this work was done with a chisel and the ridges are vertical. It very conveniently dates a building. The change-over is sometimes considered to have taken place at the end of the Norman period but at Wells and elsewhere in Somerset it continued until about 1200.

LABEL. Outside a building this is best known as a 'drip-stone'. It is a moulding in a wall following the course of a door or window on its outer edge. Its purpose was to prevent rain running down the wall and in the archway. Inside a building its use was purely decorative.

LANCET. The name given to the Early English window which had no tracery and a sharp head like a lance.

LIERNE. The name of a type of vaulting intermediate in date between the use of plain rolls or ribs in Early English, and the fan vault of the fifteenth century. The liernes are short ribs joining up the main ones.

MANIPLE. One of the Eucharistic vestments. It is a towel which later became purely ornamental, worn over the left wrist.

MISERICORDE. The under part of a choir seat, often finely carved.

MITRE. The head-wear of a bishop.

MORSE. A clasp, often jewelled, joining the front of a cope across the chest.

MULLION. The upright (usually stone) divisions of a window.

NECKING. The lower end of the capital carving, usually a ring.

ORDER. Of a window or arch. A large arch is usually first built with a single set of stones on a wooden framework. When completed it will stay up by itself. This is the first order. Another arch rather wider is then built upon this making the second order. This may be repeated, although not more than three orders are usually found.

OGEE (arch). If the lines of a lancet arch are crossed over and reversed at the apex, this type of ornament, common in the fourteenth century, is obtained.

PATERAE. A row of detached, usually square, pieces of ornament running below a cornice.

PIER. The main column of an arcade dividing aisle from nave or choir.

QUATREFOIL. An ornamental opening of four leaves.

RERE ARCH. This refers usually to windows. About 1300 quite elaborate cusped arches are found inside windows.

RESPOND. When an arcade consisting of several piers has to end against a wall a problem arises. This is usually met by placing half a pier, known as the respond, against the wall.

SALTIRE. The cross of St Andrew, patron of Wells Cathedral, on which according to tradition he suffered martyrdom.

SPANDRILS. The spaces immediately above and adjoining the arches of an arcade, window or door.

STRING COURSE. A horizontal division in a scheme of decoration, usually plain and often a single roll.

SUDERY. In mediaeval days a plain cloth which could be taken off and washed was attached to the bishop's staff, to prevent the latter getting soiled with constant use.

TREFOIL. A cusped opening of three portions (two cusps), usually at the head of a window light.

TRIFORIUM. This is the space usually behind blank arches, above the arcade of large churches and below the clerestory. It occupies the space between the vault and the roof proper of the aisles. Some writers call it a tribune in Norman churches and particularly if lit by windows from the outside.

TRIPLET. Generally refers to a group of three shafts, very often found at Wells.

TRUMEAU. The central (usually stone) division of a double doorway.

TUNICLE. The vestment of the sub-deacon, almost identical with that of the deacon, also worn by the bishop in pontificals over his alb.

TWO-CENTRED ARCH. In constructing arches on paper, portions of circles are used. For the simplest possible arch, the circle or semi-circle, only one centre is required. The simplest Gothic arch, the lancet, is made of two arcs of circles and so two centres are needed.

TYMPANUM. See Spandril.

WATER-HOLDING BASE. This is an important indication of Early English work up to about 1260. The base of a column or shaft has moulding running round it. If a ridge is higher than one of the valleys, the latter will hold water, hence the name.

INDEX